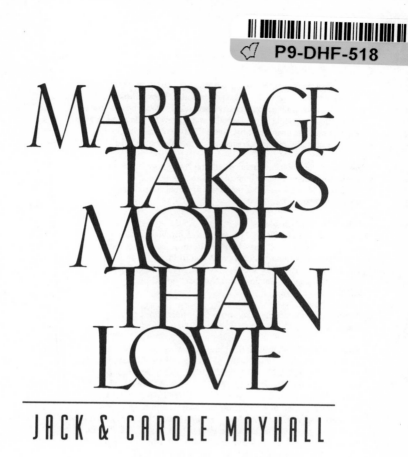

MARRIAGE TAKES MORE THAN LOVE

JACK & CAROLE MAYHALL

NAVPRESS

BRINGING TRUTH TO LIFE

NavPress Publishing Group

P.O. Box 35001, Colorado Springs, Colorado 80935

The Navigators is an international Christian organization. Our mission is to reach, disciple, and equip people to know Christ and to make Him known through successive generations. We envision multitudes of diverse people in the United States and every other nation who have a passionate love for Christ, live a lifestyle of sharing Christ's love, and multiply spiritual laborers among those without Christ.

NavPress is the publishing ministry of The Navigators. NavPress publications help believers learn biblical truth and apply what they learn to their lives and ministries. Our mission is to stimulate spiritual formation among our readers.

CONTENTS

To Lynn and Tim,
our daughter and son-in-law,
two who have become one special couple and demonstrate
. . . love in their lives,
. . . purpose in their service,
. . . eternity in their hearts.
We thank God
upon every remembrance of you.

FOREWORD

A good marriage, most people say, has no serious problems, while a poor marriage is one in which there are many problems. Not so, we believe. Problems go along with people—in and out of marriage. If you don't have problems, you're probably paralyzed.

The difference between smooth sailing and shipwreck in marriage lies in what you as a couple are doing about the rough weather. All marriages have strengths and weaknesses. All marriages are either dynamic or they are deteriorating. The husband-wife combo must either progress or perish.

Volumes have been written on why marriages fail, but only a trickle of helpful advice on the care and cultivation of good relationships has reached the bookshelves. Many couples are frustrated and despairing because they do not know how to reverse the downward trend in their lives together.

Jack and Carole Mayhall have written *Marriage Takes More Than Love* from rich personal experience to help revitalize marriages, fresh or stale. Their key is "working at it." But how? By pointing out individual responsibility, by reinforcing these concepts with scriptural principles, and by illustrating their workability from their own lives.

Overseas missionaries report that the distinctively Christian home is what makes the greatest impact on a pagan culture. Western culture, once Christian, thirsts deeply for the return of this purifying core of home life. This book points toward that goal.

—Howard and Jeanne Hendricks

PREFACE

Speaking of kissing! We weren't, of course, but let's. When our daughter was five, she had a whole repertoire of kisses. She had the eyelash-against-cheek "butterfly," the rub-noses "Eskimo," the starting-at-oneside-around-face-to-other-side "sliding" kiss, and the old-fashioned "smack."

Such diversity also exists today in describing marriages, ranging from happy to good to mediocre to awful to hopeless. But only a small percent claim the "happy" label. A few more hope for "good," but most openly admit it is a pretty ghastly marriage-go-round they're riding.

Today the marriage picture looks so dark that light and shadow have little contrast on the screen. We don't wonder why so many marriages fall apart; rather, we are amazed that any hang together.

Forces seem to be striking us over which we have no control. And the more prophets of doom shriek around us, the more obsessed we become with our own failures and inadequacies.

But GOD . . . !

It is a fact that the divorce rate in the United States of America is at the 50 percent mark. We see around us a degenerating society lapping up the salt water of self-destruction, trying to satisfy an unquenchable thirst for something always just beyond reach. We hear story after story of broken relationships, unhappy homes, and miserable marriages.

But GOD . . . !

It takes three persons to make a satisfying marriage. A husband, a wife, and God. Marriage can be a beautiful, deeply satisfying, fulfilling relationship. But only because God is in it.

God created, designed, and planned marriage. He then initiated a plan to ensure that it would work. That plan, given in the Bible and in the book of Ephesians, is called the "walk" of the Christian. Biblically, this "walk" is how a Christian is to live day by day, progressing one obedient step at a time and listening carefully to God's voice as He speaks through His Word. Apart from that walk—obeying God in our lives—a lasting, loving relationship is incredibly difficult to achieve.

But with God's leading and help, as two people progress and grow in love, a happy marriage is a cinch . . . well, not quite a cinch. It does take two essential ingredients forever and always.

One ingredient is prayer, for without God's power this walk in love is impossible.

The other is a determination on the part of both to work at this relationship. Marriage cannot be put on autopilot.

Committed to these ingredients, any couple can build a relationship that reflects Christ's love for His Church.

This is a "his and hers" book. We hope that you will read it together as an engaged or married couple, so we present it from two points of view. A "his and hers" view. You will find the outlooks different. But we trust you will find one essential message.

Since writing this book in 1978, we've continued to grow as a couple. In His faithfulness, God has continued to teach us how to love Himself and each other more completely.

We've expanded and revised *Marriage Takes More Than Love* to include some of what He's taught us since then. In addition, we've added portions of a previous book, *Opposites Attack*, to include more insight on loving each other—even when you're completely different.

It is our prayer that some of the things God has taught us in the last forty plus years of knowing one another will help you fall more deeply in love with each other and with the God who created us all.

PART ONE

THE BASIS FOR A SUCCESSFUL MARRIAGE

CHAPTER ONE

CHOOSING A FOUNDATION

by Jack

I glanced up from the tennis court to where Carole was watching and grinned. We exchanged a wink and a glance that said, "Hi. I'm glad you're here. Thanks for being you."

As I resumed play, I thought of the numerous times we have shared such moments. Many years ago it was a football field instead of a tennis court. Aware of Carole yelling encouragement from the stands of our small college, I would look up and wave. Through the years the scene has changed from basketball courts to handball courts to tennis courts.

These have been moments of sharing that have soldered intimacy to the framework of our lives. Carole and I have deliberately chosen to share these moments together.

All of marriage is a choice. One small choice follows on the heels of another till the trail becomes clear and worn. The right choices make for intimacy and closeness—a oneness in marriage that equals no other relationship on the human level. Wrong choices start a couple on the road to disenchantment and loneliness, emotional—and perhaps physical—separation. One such choice is not conscious for most of us. Yet it is even more important than the choice of a partner for life. It is deciding the foundation on which the marriage will rest.

I am not sure that Carole and I ever gave conscious thought to this foundation. We met, fell in love, dated in college for three-and-a-half years, got engaged, unengaged, engaged again (we had a rather stormy time of it and broke our engagement three times), and finally walked down the aisle in a woodframe church in a small Michigan town. I was a bit late for the wedding, the best man lost the wedding ring (his wife found it a few minutes after the ceremony), but nothing could rob us of that moment we had been anticipating for so long.

We had not thought through goals and objectives, or what we really wanted our marriage and our lives to be based on. However, we had a number of things going for us. Love was exemplified in both our home backgrounds. We observed a great deal in the lives of our parents without being actively aware of what deep truths we were learning. As children, both of us had invited Jesus Christ to come into our lives, to be our Lord and Savior. And we had begun to experience Christ leading us day by day.

Each of us had prayed for some time, and we knew our parents had long prayed as well, concerning God's choice of a life-partner. When we said, "I do," we were confident that God had answered those prayers.

Finally, we knew the truth of the psalmist's statement, "Unless the LORD builds the house, they labor in vain who build it" (Psalm 127:1). God builds that "house" from scratch.

MARRIAGE IS GOD'S IDEA

The great foundation stone of marriage was dug and firmly laid in place at the creation of the world. People may think that marriage was their idea, but they are wrong.

Genesis is the book of beginnings, and records the story of the creation in the first chapter. When God finished each day's work, He surveyed the world and declared, "It is good!" But on the sixth day, when man and woman were created, God looked out over His vast creation and said, "It is *very* good!" (Genesis 1:31, emphasis added).

That says something to me. God wasn't just a little pleased with the job He had done in creating man and woman. He was enormously satisfied. When God leads two people together, puts a love in their hearts for each other, and joins them in the bond of marriage, that is a unique creation. The touch of God's hand is on that new relationship.

In the second chapter of Genesis, God gives us some insights into the details of what happened on that momentous sixth day. In a beautiful account, He explains how Adam and Eve got together.

Use your imagination and picture the Garden of Eden. I don't know what the Garden of Eden would be for you (our pictures will probably be different), but for me it would have at least two eighteen-hole golf courses (Robert Trent Jones designed), beautifully laid out.

Adam was in a paradise that was everything his heart could desire in terms of beauty and satisfaction. He had it made. He even had the privilege of taking walks with God. Yes, the Lord Himself walked with Adam.

Yet as God looked into the heart of this man whom He had created, He saw something there that caused Him to ponder. Something was missing. So God said, "He's lonely. He is all alone. I will make for him a helper fit for him" (see Genesis 2:18). (Not a helper to give him fits, but a helper fit for him!)

A great search began. "Out of the ground the LORD God formed every beast of the field and every bird of the sky, and brought them to the man to see what he would call them; and whatever the man called a living creature, that was its name. [*Note:* Can you imagine how long that would have taken if Eve had been on the scene? They might still have been at it!] . . . But for Adam there was not found a helper suitable [or fit] for him" (2:19-20).

God and Adam looked everywhere, but they didn't find anything that would meet his need. "So the LORD God caused a deep sleep to fall upon the man, and he slept; then He took one of his ribs, and closed up the flesh at that place. And the LORD God fashioned into a woman the rib which He had taken from the man, and brought her to the man. And the man said, 'This is now bone of my bones, and flesh of my flesh; she shall be called Woman, because she was taken out of Man'" (2:21-23).

Can you put yourself into that situation? There was Adam in these beautiful surroundings. He was still rubbing sleep from his eyes when all of a sudden, out of the trees, walked a gorgeous creature. He had never seen one like this before; he had never seen a woman. And he got excited about it. He may have let out a long whistle and yelled out, "Wow! At last!" He was thoroughly impressed.

And that was the start of marriage, for the passage goes on, "For this cause a man shall leave his father and his mother, and shall cleave to his wife; and they shall become one flesh" (2:24). This command is repeated three other times in the Bible, that a man shall leave, and cleave, and the two shall become one flesh (Matthew 19:5, Mark 10:7-8, Ephesians 5:31). Marriage is God's idea. It was His creative plan and He made it beautiful. It is man who has disfigured and marred it, but it need not be so.

MARRIAGE CAN BE SUCCESSFUL

Most of us want to be successful in our marriages. We don't get married determined to fail. A national survey once indicated that 80 percent of Americans over age eighteen choose "a happy family life" as their number one goal. A happy family life was selected over the opportunity to develop as an individual, or a fulfilling career, or making money. Some 75 percent of the respondents also agreed with the statement, "The traditional family is important to American society and should be preserved."

We live in an age which provides an atmosphere that causes most married couples to have almost everything going against them for success. Yet the Apostle Paul's statement, "If God is for us, who is against us?" (Romans 8:31), is as true today as when it was written.

God is still in the business of creating marriages. He desires to be the foundation stone of each union. Most marriages are based on nothing; it is not surprising that many collapse.

But it is never too late with God. At any point, if we turn over our lives and our marriages to Him, He will become the foundation, the builder, and the rebuilder, if that is necessary, of that home. Even the broken pieces of our lives can be mended and repaired if we let God be God in every area of our human relationships.

CHAPTER TWO

CHOOSING GOD AS LORD

by Carole

I t happened in the middle of one of the three times Jack and I had broken our engagement. I was miserable. Miserable because Jack's ring was no longer on my finger. But even more unhappy because I had lost the feeling of God's presence. With anxiety and tears I sought the Lord time after time, asking Him for His comfort and peace. My prayers seemed to ricochet off the light fixture, bounce off the desk, and lie in a miserable heap at my feet. I wasn't getting through.

I said, "Lord, what's the matter? I need You now more than ever before. Don't You hear me? Please tell me what is wrong."

And He got through to me.

Since becoming one of His children, I had assured God that if He wanted me to be single, I would be willing. And I meant it. However, that was before I fell in love with Jack. Subtly the picture had changed. I couldn't view life without Jack anymore. I felt that if God didn't give Jack to me, my life would be second-rate at best.

But God would have no rival in my life. He was teaching me a deep spiritual lesson through this experience of heartache. Finally, as I cried and prayed, He convinced me that His will was perfect; it was best for me. If marrying Jack was His second best, would I really want that for my life?

I struggled with that one for a while because it was hard for me to conceive that life with Jack could be second best. At last I surrendered my will to God and said, "Whatever is Your first best for me, Father, whatever will bring You the most glory even if it means being single for the rest of my life, that is what I want. Please help me want Your will in my life above everything else. Help me want more of You because I know that only You can truly satisfy."

In that moment, I felt as though the ceiling and roof rolled away and I had direct access to heaven itself! God's presence, His comfort, and His peace shoved my empty spiritual gauge to FULL.

A few months later, God led us together again—permanently this time, for which I have been forever grateful. A lasting lesson seared my heart that day, which burned the knowledge on my mind that no human being, no matter how wonderful, can satisfy the longings of the human heart. Only God can do that. There really is a God-shaped vacuum in every human heart that only God can fill.

God has blessed me with a loving and tender husband. Jack is all that I could ask for in a mate. God has also given us a daughter who is walking with Him and is now married to a wonderful man. They continually rejoice our hearts. But even with these and all the other blessings of life, an emptiness and futility would remain within except for God.

I have seen too many wives try to force their husbands to meet their every need—a feat no human can do—and in the forcing have destroyed what could have been a beautiful relationship.

God meant a husband and a wife to be two whole, complete individuals. Complete in Him. When these two complete individuals, having their needs met by God Himself, come together in a marriage designed by Him, they equal more than two. They multiply to four or eight or a hundred. I don't mean children. I mean the impact of their lives and ministries. But if we marry as only a part of a person, and then depend on our mates for survival, we become parasites that feed on the other spouse, draining our own lives of joy and fulfillment.

It took me a while to learn this. Jack has always been a good "need-meeter." It wasn't till a change in jobs caused him to travel almost half the time that I finally learned a needed lesson.

At first, when Jack was away and couldn't meet my needs, I became dissatisfied and frustrated. Then God began to teach me a deep truth about Himself. He really meant it when He said that He could and would satisfy my every need. He began to be my Companion, my Comfort, and my Joy in a new way.

Only the puzzle pieces were not fitting together. One time when Jack was home, he said to me, "Sometimes I get the feeling that I'm not needed around here anymore!"

My heart sank. What a terrible impression to leave with the one I love most on this earth. I immediately made some "set apart" time to ask God about that one. And God put the jigsaw pieces together in my thinking.

Yes, God alone meets my needs. But when He gave Jack to me, He chose to meet those needs, many times, through my husband. At other times, He meets them through my daughter, Lynn, or relatives or friends. When He chooses to meet my need of companionship, comfort, tenderness, joy through my husband or others, He will do it in no other way. So I am totally dependent on Jack at that time. However, if Jack can't (or in a very few cases, won't) meet my needs, there is no cause for frustration or unhappiness. Because God can and will meet those needs! He is reaching out to meet the needs of our hearts.

A sign on a church bulletin board read, "God can mend a broken heart, if you will give Him all the pieces." God can also mend a broken marriage . . . if you will give Him all the pieces. He can take a shattered marriage and glue it together so perfectly that it will not even show the cracks. He will make it stronger than it was before it shattered. Or He can take a good marriage and make it more beautiful every day.

The secret lies in giving it all to Him. And before that can be done with a marriage, it has to be done by the individuals that form the marriage. Perhaps the greatest prayer a wife or husband can pray is, "Lord, save this marriage, beginning with me!" Or, "Change this marriage, beginning with me!"

James Jauncey, an eminent Australian educator, said:

> Many women have asked wistfully: "Why could it not always be like when we were first married?" Well, it can. The newness and the excitement die down, of course, and the emotional froth subsides somewhat. Couples tend to get used to anything in time. But a deep romantic love can continue as if the soul is being fed by some inner springs. If you have lost that love, the fountain hasn't dried up. You have ceased to tap it, that's all.
>
> This is true not only of marriage, but of life itself. Every thing about living can begin to pall unless we have hidden resources to replenish what is being depleted. All of life was intended to be a vibrant experience.[1]

We have to tap that resource. God is the source of love, of understanding, of acceptance. As we put our roots down deeply into Him, there flows into us a never-ending supply (see Isaiah 37:31, Jeremiah 17:7-8). Walter Trobisch, European pastor, teacher, and missionary to Africa, says that "love is a feeling to be learned,"[2] and this is true. We have to learn to love — really love — and we learn it from God.

I've had women tell me that they have lost all feeling for their husbands; all respect, all love. They feel helpless and trapped and so they would be, without the power and strength of the Source. He alone can teach us to love deeply, in the way that we long to love the person to whom we are married.

But it has to begin with me. I cannot change my husband, but I can let the God of the universe change me. And in changing me into the kind of wife, the kind of person He wants me to be, my marriage will inevitably be altered.

I am not just half a couple. I am a complete child of God united with another complete child of God. And this is such a wondrous thing that nothing on earth comes close to it. With God as our unshakable foundation, our love will endure forever.

"So overflowing is his kindness towards us that he took away all our sins through the blood of his Son, by whom we are saved; and he has showered down upon us the richness of his grace — for how well he understands us and knows what is best for us at all times" (Ephesians 1:7-9, TLB).

Notes

1. From *Magic in Marriage* by James H. Jauncey, p. 9. Copyright © 1966 by Zondervan Publishing House, Grand Rapids, Mich. Used by permission.
2. Walter Trobisch, *Love Is a Feeling to Be Learned* (copyright © 1971 by Editions Trobisch, D-737 Baden Baden, Germany; published by InterVarsity Press, Downers Grove, Ill.), p. 9.

CHAPTER THREE

CHOOSING THE ARCHITECT

by Jack

T hat Saturday morning in March was one of those spectacular warm days we get in Colorado in late winter. It had been an unusually long, cold season, and as I glanced out the window toward Pike's Peak, the 14,000-foot mountain that overlooks the city, I thought, *What a perfect day for my first golf game this year!* By the time I had shaved and dressed, I was so psyched up for that golf game, I could think of little else than to be out there on the golf course.

Carole, still not being able to read my thoughts after all these years of marriage, prepared a nice breakfast. Then, as we sat down to eat, she remarked, "Honey, it's such a beautiful day [I certainly agreed with that], wouldn't it be fun to go on a picnic and take a hike?"

I didn't say a word. But I thought, *Now that has got to be the dumbest idea she ever thought up.*

The day suddenly didn't look so good after all. I got moody, grumpy, and silent. And Carole didn't even know what had happened.

I didn't tell her what was going on in my mind; instead, I pouted inside for hours. I ruined the day. We didn't go on a picnic, and I didn't play golf. Early in the afternoon, God finally got through to me and showed me what a DRA (in our household that stands for Dirty Rotten Attitude) I was having. And God called it by name—sin. He called it that because that is exactly what it was. I was being selfish, unkind, and mean.

Finally, I confessed it to God, asked Carole's forgiveness, and we managed to salvage a part of that day by spending some time together.

DEMONSTRATING LOVE

It is not always easy to demonstrate love, to be kind, to respond as Christ would. And the most difficult place to do this is at home.

The Apostle Paul, in his beautiful letter to the Ephesians, talks about three major subjects: the wealth (1:1–3:20), the walk (4:1–6:10), and the warfare (6:11-24) of a Christian. First, Paul tells us of the wealth that we possess simply by being children of God through Jesus Christ. Then he talks about how Christians are to live their daily lives. He concludes by telling us of the warfare against Satan in which we are constantly engaged. The key passage about the marriage relationship comes, not in the warfare section as some might think, but right in the center of the discussion on what it means to walk as a believer.

One of the goals God has for us—our walk in Christ—is for us to grow up in Him, to become mature people (4:13). The important ingredients for that maturity are the characteristics of kindness, understanding, and forgiveness; Paul states clearly, "Be kind to one another, tender-hearted, forgiving each other, just as God in Christ also has forgiven you" (4:32).

Our Christian life, then, is to be a walk of love, which is learning to respond to each other in a continually loving way (5:2), and a walk of wisdom, which is growing in the understanding and discernment of Jesus Christ (5:15). Now if there are any two things that we need to make a successful marriage, it is love and wisdom; and these come only from God.

BEING FILLED WITH THE HOLY SPIRIT

The Apostle Paul continues and commands his readers—the Ephesians and us—to be "filled with the Spirit" (5:18). Without going into a theological treatise on this, being filled with the Spirit means that we let the Holy Spirit of God control how we act and what we say; we let Him have His way in our lives.

Sometimes that is extremely difficult. Being filled with the Spirit may not seem so hard when we are preparing for a Sunday school class, for a Bible study group, or a message. Most of us are unsure of ourselves in situations like these and fully aware that we cannot do them in our own strength. We have no choice but to pray that God will take over for us, and He does.

But when our guards are down, like in our own homes, it can be another story. Because life is so daily, many things come up in its course that make it difficult for us to act like Christians, especially toward those we love the most.

On that beautiful Saturday morning in March when I wanted to play golf, my guard was down and the enemy of my soul got off a shot that pierced my armor. I was anything but "filled with the Spirit."

I spoke in the opening session of a large conference in California shortly after moving to Colorado, and I felt totally inadequate for the situation. I prayed a great deal about it and had many others praying for me as well. I asked the Lord to speak through me, and the whole conference went beautifully. The Lord blessed it, using my message in the lives of many.

Then I got home.

We had moved into a new house three months before, and winter by now had set in. We had to install a new humidifier on the furnace. (In Colorado it is so dry that unless you put humidity in the air, the static electricity is so bad that every time you kiss your wife, the sparks really *do* fly.) When we returned home, the humidifier had leaked all over the floor into the furnace, which was now standing in a couple of inches of water.

That night, a snowstorm blew in from the north, our first since moving into that house. We have double doors that face north. The next morning we got up and found that we had almost enough snow in our hallway to make a snowman. Well, a few snowballs at least! Now a door just isn't supposed to do that.

Yes, there are times when it is very difficult to be filled with the Spirit.

BUILDING A MARRIAGE

All kinds of daily situations come up in our lives which affect our relationships with one another as husband and wife and cause us to cast ourselves on the Lord. On these, "the dailies of life," as Carole calls them, rest the balance of the scales. To respond as one who is filled with the Spirit weights the "happy marriage" side; to respond in our own flesh may put the balance on "miserable."

I really don't know anything about building houses. And I'd be a fool to build a house without a competent architect planning every board for me.

I don't know that much about building marriages either— and I only intend to build one. I would be a greater fool not to let the Creator of marriage be my Architect. He wants to make a beautiful creation from each relationship given to Him. But He won't force His services on us. He waits to be asked. Right responses are only possible if we allow God to be in complete control. His Spirit alone can and will give us victory in areas where we are weak and defenseless.

A growing relationship with God and turning your marriage over to Him as Resident Architect and Builder will result in His helping you respond as one "filled with the Spirit" in the daily affairs of life.

PART TWO

UNDERSTANDING
ONE ANOTHER

CHAPTER FOUR

CHOOSING TO UNDERSTAND

by Carole

J ack appeared in the doorway just as I breezed in the back door and set a bag of groceries on the kitchen table. He was wearing a blue shirt and a peculiar look which I could not read. He said, "Please come upstairs. I need to talk to you."

Now? How strange! I thought. Wondering, I followed him up the stairs, leaving the groceries to be unpacked later.

As we sat on the bed, Jack took both my hands in his. "Before I tell you something, I'd like to remind you of a verse in Psalms," he said. "The verse is Psalm 115:3, 'Our God is in the heavens: he hath done whatsoever he hath pleased'" (KJV).

Growing increasingly more puzzled, I nodded.

He continued, "Your mother just called. Dad is in the hospital with acute leukemia. The doctors . . ." and his voice broke. "You have reservations on a plane leaving in two hours. I have already arranged for Lynn to be cared for."

Then he put his arms around me and held me tight.

I was numb. Yet strangely not unprepared. A few weeks before, God had impressed a verse on my heart as I was reading His Word, which said, "He shall not be afraid of evil tidings: his heart is fixed, trusting in the LORD" (Psalm 112:7, KJV). I felt God was telling me that something was going to happen soon for which I needed to be spiritually prepared. However, I hadn't dreamed that my robust fifty-seven-year-old father would be stricken.

Two hours later I was on a plane eastward bound. Finances prevented Jack from accompanying me, and I felt very much alone.

The next ten days blurred together. Daddy grew worse rapidly, caught pneumonia, and died five days after my arrival. The burial arrangements, the funeral, the grief, the sustaining grace of God, His comfort and peace, packing, bringing Mother back to the coast with me all telescoped together through the lens of sorrow.

Then I was home. Jack met us, and after getting Mother settled in the guest room, he took me out in our little VW. Parking in a quiet spot off the road, he turned to comfort me.

An unbidden thought flashed through my mind. *How can you comfort me?* it grumbled. *You weren't there. You can't know what I've been through. You can't really understand.* And my heart was cold. I pulled the tattered edges of my grief to me and hugged them in loneliness and self-pity.

But God would not allow it. In one brief second, I had to make a choice to shut Jack out because I thought he couldn't totally understand or to share this thing together.

Deliberately, by an act of my will, I put my wounded spirit in the hands of Jack's concern to be bandaged with his love.

Many forks occur in our marriage roads—choices which lead us together or tear us apart. Later, I realized this was one of them—the sharing of pain, sorrow, and grief, or the shutting out of the other because I thought he could not understand completely.

At Lynn's birth, Jack couldn't actually feel the bearing down pains as I labored to bring her into the world, but he shared them. I couldn't have made it through those forty-eight hours without his strength and comfort. In one way, I think he suffered more than I.

The intense pain that bathed his body in perspiration within seconds after a kidney stone attack made me want to writhe in empathy, but all I could do was race him to the hospital. He bore the pain, but we shared the experience.

That's what it is all about. Choosing to share and to understand.

But it isn't easy to understand.

One of Charles Schulz's Peanuts cartoons illustrates our dilemma.

I have to sympathize with Charlie Brown. We have so much understanding to do that I sometimes feel "I don't even understand what it is I don't understand."

All of us view others from a biased point of view. We can't help comparing another's actions and responses with how we would have acted or responded. When we fail to see things through another's eyes, when we have no understanding, then inevitably a different response than our own would be comes out a wrong response.

J. B. Phillips paraphrases Ephesians 4:32 this way: "Be kind to one another; be understanding. Be as ready to forgive others as God for Christ's sake has forgiven you."

Be kind.

Be understanding.

Be forgiving. Not just a little forgiving. But as much as God for Christ's sake has already forgiven you. How much is that? Everything. Totally. A good marriage is simply the union of "two awfully good forgivers." Yet forgiveness is hard. One man said, "When we quarrel, my wife becomes historical."

His friend replied, "Don't you mean hysterical?"

"No," the first replied, "I mean historical. She reminds me of everything I ever did to her."

To forgive is to put the offense away completely. Real forgiveness requires strength and love from God . . . and it is not optional.

Many times we don't want to forgive, for if we do we become vulnerable to be hurt all over again. So we build walls of resentment and unforgiveness in protecting ourselves from recurring pain. Logically this makes some kind of sense. But emotionally it poisons, above all, the person with the unforgiving heart.

David Augsburger, radio speaker for "The Mennonite Hour," put it this way:

> Forgiveness is hard. Especially in a marriage tense with past troubles, tormented by fears of rejection and humiliation, and torn by suspicion and distrust.
>
> Forgiveness hurts. Especially when it must be extended to a husband or wife who doesn't deserve it, who hasn't earned it, who may misuse it. It hurts to forgive.
>
> Forgiveness costs. Especially in a marriage when it means accepting instead of demanding repayment for the wrong done; where it means releasing the other instead of exacting revenge; where it means reaching out in love instead of relinquishing resentments. It costs to forgive.[1]

He later explains that, stated psychologically, forgiveness takes place when the person who was offended and justly angered by the offender bears his own anger, and lets the other go free.

> Anger cannot be ignored, denied, or forgotten without doing treachery in hidden ways. It must be dealt with responsibly, honestly, in a decisive act of the will. Either the injured and justifiably angry person vents his feelings on the other in retaliation—(that is an attempt at achieving justice as accuser, judge, and hangman all in one)—or the injured person may choose to accept his angry feelings, bear the burden of them personally, find release through confession and prayer and set the other person free. This is forgiveness.[2]

This is what Jesus Christ did for us. He forgave us unconditionally, bearing the burden, setting us free. "In Him we have
redemption through His blood, the forgiveness of our trespasses,
according to the riches of His grace, which He lavished upon us"
(Ephesians 1:7-8; see 1 Peter 2:24).

We're not talking about the steps which sometimes must be
taken when a person violates our trust, is abusive, or steps over
our "line of respect." We're talking about an attitude of the heart
out of obedience to God.

But directly in the middle of this verse in Ephesians in the
Phillips paraphrase, between kindness and forgiveness, comes the
phrase, "Be understanding."

Most of us have little or no real understanding of one another.
And it takes a "heap of understanding" to make a marriage.

It is a lifelong project to learn to understand each other. But
only in understanding is true love. If you can figure out the person with whom you are living, everything else will be easy by com-
parison.

I have to understand Jack's background, his idiosyncrasies, his
introvert leanings, his personality, how he views and interacts with
the world around him, his thinking. He has to do the same with
me. To know him that completely, I have to study him.

Mrs. Norman Vincent Peale puts her finger right on this area:

> If I could give one piece of advice to young brides, and
> only one, it would be this: study your man. Study him as if
> he were some rare and strange and fascinating animal,
> which he is. Study his likes and dislikes, his strengths and
> weaknesses, his moods and mannerisms. Just loving a man
> is fine, but it's not enough. To live with one successfully
> you have to know him, and to know him, you have to
> study him. Look around you and decide how many of the
> best marriages you know are ones where a wife in a deep
> sense actually knows her husband better than he knows

himself. Knows what pleases him. Knows what upsets him. Knows what makes him laugh or makes him angry. Knows when he needs encouragement. Knows when he's too charged up about something and needs to be held back. Knows, in other words, exactly what makes him tick.[3]

For years I never really studied Jack. I was much like the bride of seven weeks I talked with a while ago. It had been a hectic two weeks for her and she felt they really were not communicating. At last they had a few moments alone one Sunday afternoon and were lying on the bed with her head on his shoulder.

After a long, poignant silence, she asked, "What are you thinking?" (Men, if your wife ever asks you that question in those circumstances, please be thinking about her.)

This one wasn't. Instead, his choice answer was, "Oh, I was just wondering what I should tell the boss tomorrow when he asks me about that project I've been working on."

She said, "Oh!"

Then she waited. Now any man with a grain of knowledge about the working of most women's minds would have known she was waiting for him to ask her what she was thinking.

This one didn't. Instead, he asked, "Are you going to fix supper pretty soon?"

Between clenched teeth she flatly monotoned, "Maybe in a little while."

"Well," he offered cheerily, "I'll be glad to teach you how to fix cheese-dogs." With that innocent offer, the lid blew off her anger. He thought, *What did I say to make her so angry? She is being unreasonable!*

She thought, *This man I married doesn't have the sensitivity of a frog!*

This bride related that incident to me several weeks after it happened. She had never told her husband what was really on her mind that Sunday afternoon. As a result of this one incident, their marriage very quickly had begun going in two directions—his way and her way, 180° away from each other. She was getting angry more often because she felt totally misunderstood. He continued thinking he had married an unhappy and frustrated woman.

My friend needed one of three things to handle that situation—if not all three. She needed humor, to laugh at herself, at him, at the situation (but a bride of seven weeks seldom can do that).

Or, she needed openness, to be able to say honestly, "Hey, that hurt. I wanted you to be thinking about me, because I'm feeling romantic right now and quite vulnerable because we haven't had a chance to talk the last two weeks."

Or, she needed to understand that her husband was put together on a quite different frequency than she. When he was thinking about business instead of thinking about her, it was not a sign that he didn't love her deeply (which was the first thing that came to her mind).

My friend had neither humor, nor openness, nor understanding. Like me in those early years, she had not begun to study her husband.

True understanding is a lifelong project. A day . . . a week . . . a year of study will not suffice. The rich reward of deep sharing, clear understanding, total love is won only by devoting an entire life to praying and working toward those goals. Each of us is constantly changing. Study that change with wonder. Determine with God's help to choose to understand.

Notes
1. David W. Augsburger, *Cherishable: Love and Marriage* (Scottsdale, Penn.: Herald Press, 1971), pp. 141-142.
2. Augsburger, p. 144.
3. Mrs. Norman Vincent Peale, *The Adventure of Being a Wife* (Englewood Cliffs, N.J.: Prentice-Hall, Inc., 1971), p. 29.

CHAPTER FIVE

CHOOSING TO KNOW

by Carole

J ack and Carole Mayhall. Color us different.

Color Jack's hair red. Frost it with gray. Paint on eyes—deep brown.

Color Carole's eyes blue, speckled with green. Hair: brown. (Please paint out the gray.)

But don't stop with the outward.

Peel off the surface layers and color us totally different inside too. Through the years the colors have muted and blended in some areas of personality. But they will forever be individual.

Vive la différence!

God gave us two eyes to see things from a slightly different point of view. If we have only one eye, we lose perspective. We see things flat, rather than round. We lose some of the wonder of the world around us.

God created couples with slightly different points of view for the same reason. We will have a better view of the world, a better understanding of people, and more perspective if we use both points of view.

But to use our differences, we have to understand them, and then to accept them. As we talk to couples, we find very few who have begun to do this. Our differences, accepted and appreciated, are God's way of making us fit together as a couple so that we will be stronger together than either of us could be apart. Jack's strengths compensate for my weaknesses and my gifts supplement areas in which he is lacking. As some of our differences are explained, God's creativity in distinctives is evident.

Jack is an objective person. To him a fact is a fact is a fact is a fact. He often takes a detached view of life and his perspective is broad. He thinks in concepts rather than in particulars.

Not me. I have a difficult time being objective or detached about anything. From my point of view, a fact is never a cold, hard fact, but a little bit more than or a fraction less than a fact depending on my frame of mind.

There is one big hole in the fabric of Jack's objectivity, however, and that hole is me. He can turn subjective in a split second when I come on in a negative way concerning something he has said or done. Because I love him, I need to understand this exception. I need to be sensitive to his sensitivity.

With my subjective nature, I take teasing very poorly. Even if Jack grins reassuringly when he calls me "Chubby" (if he calls me "Chubby"), I will be positive he is telling me I am immersed in rolls of fat. And even if that were true, I couldn't take being reminded by a barb even if it was in jest.

If Jack remarks, "The Joneses are busy and can't come tomorrow," I'll think, *I wonder if we've offended them?*

I even identify with this incident where subjectivity borders on the ridiculous.

A man said to his wife, "Honey, you've been working so hard all week, cooking, cleaning, and taking care of the kids. Tonight I'm going to take you out for a good dinner."

And his wife burst into tears!

For you who didn't get it, she had picked up on the "good dinner." What had she been cooking for him all week? Bad meals? Earlier in my married life, I could have been seriously hurt by a kind, generous offer such as that one. Not any more. Now I realize that Jack would be making a thoughtful offer and would in no way be making a derogatory remark about the nature of my meals.

Knowing my own nature helps me work on being more understanding and at trying to take a more objective approach. But often when my head tells me not to take something personally, my heart still says, "Ouch!" I am now trying to get my heart and my head all connected up right.

Jack, on the other hand, understands my emotions better all the time. He tries to be very careful about teasing and I appreciate him for it. I have to accept Jack's objectivity and he has to accept my subjective nature. Neither are wrong; they are just different. But we have to know these things about one another.

Another big difference in us is that I have a mind which grooves on details while Jack goes right to the essential point of a matter. This has many implications in our relationship. It has caused me to feel he wasn't interested in my conversation, wasn't interested in telling me about his job, and even, at times, made me feel he wasn't interested in people. None of which is true.

Often he would go to a week-long conference and, on arriving home, find me waiting to hear all about it. So he would tell me all about it — in ten minutes flat. I would think, *He doesn't care enough to tell me about the conference.* Yet from his point of view, he had told me all about that conference. He had zeroed in on the essential points of the week. I had wanted to hear all the details. We both ended up frustrated and sometimes angry due to different thinking processes.

I am learning that it is so much more important to think together than to think alike. We are different. We will always remain so. We are learning to accept and understand these differences. I am no longer hurt when he tells me all about a conference in ten minutes. (However, I have learned how to ask the right questions to ferret out details that I want to know. And he has learned to jot down who is going to have babies, who is engaged, and what was the best meal he had.)

Being detail-minded helps me to do several things at once. I can be cooking lasagna, talking on the telephone, letting the dog out, and planning a party all at the same time. Jack's concentration is distracted by interruptions as he concentrates on one thing at a time. Not wrong. Just different.

Have you ever started to tell a man like Jack about your next door neighbor, the one whose husband ran for the Senate, whose secretary was divorced last year . . . you know, the one who had the maiden aunt who was in a sanitarium for a while last year, and . . . ? Suddenly you glance at your husband and his eyes are glazed over and sort of crossed. You think, *He's not listening to me.* And you're right. You lost him four details ago.

Before I understood more of Jack's thinking processes, at this point I would think, *Oh, if he isn't listening, then he's not interested. If he's not interested in what I am saying, he must not be interested in me. Therefore, how could he love me the way I long to be loved?*

Consciously or subconsciously, my mind works that way. Criticism, inference, even a difference of opinion can set my mind on my own private pilgrimage, which ends with, *He must not love me the way I long to be loved.* I need constant reassurance of Jack's love, which fortunately he understands and gives me.

My mind for details leads me to be impressed by and often distracted by a lot of little things — the accidental and the incidental. Jack will say, "That's a good-looking car, but how does it run?" (the essential).

I'll say, "I just don't care for the color" (the detail).

Jack may say, "This is a well-constructed house."

And then I will comment, "The view from the bedroom is spectacular."

Not wrong. Just different.

Now before you wonder how we've managed to stay together for so many years, I want to show how beautifully God fit Jack and me together, to make us stronger and for us to help each other.

It has been said that "intuition" is more than a feeling with no basis. Someone has suggested that it is rather a mind for detail which gives birth to a feeling.

Jack and I can go into a situation and have different vibes about it. When we come away, often he asks how I felt about it. When I tell him, he shakes his head in wonder. But a great many times I'm right.

What has happened? I have picked up twenty little details that I am unaware of noticing—a tone of voice, a raised eyebrow, a posture. They have been filtered into the computer of my mind and come back to me as a feeling, an intuition if you will. Jack takes that feeling, filters it through his objective grid, and investigates. He comes away with a much better perspective than if either of us saw that situation alone. We fit together.

Jack needs my detail-oriented mind, and I certainly need his ability to see the essentials and to be objective in situations where I respond emotionally. I can sense how people are reacting faster than Jack can and he uses this.

Jack tends to be much more logical in his thinking process. He will study the evidence and, in a step-by-step reasoning process, reach a conclusion. I rely much more on intuition, instinct, and emotion to reach the conclusion, many times the same one (and my way is faster, too).

I was talking to a friend of mine who said she was going to sign up for a course in conversation. When I asked her why she was planning to take such a course, as she is an enthusiastic, interesting person already, she said her husband gets angry at her for not "talking straight." He says she doesn't say what she means in a direct way.

I wished her luck with the course, and told her if it worked, I'd join the next one.

I am most grateful for a husband who doesn't get irritated at the way I think and talk.

Jack, being logical, thinks in straight lines and talks that way too; direct, to the point, no frills. I think more in circles, and talk in circles at times as well. Now this is something I am working on, but in which I will never be proficient. I'm sure it has something to do with the sensitivity part of me. In other words, unless I sneak up on a subject, rather than hitting it head-on, I might get hurt . . . or hurt you. For instance, you might hear the following conversation around our house fifteen minutes before we are to go out to dinner.

> CAROLE: I suppose I really ought to change.
> JACK: Well, why don't you? (Zoom! To the point!)
> CAROLE: Don't you like what I've got on?
> JACK: It's okay, but you said you were going to change.
> CAROLE: I was just saying that to see if it was all right not to.
> JACK: (Looks baffled and shakes his head.)

It is complicated living with most of us. I even have trouble understanding me.

All mixed up in the above is the way Jack and I use speech. Jack speaks to convey facts and ideas. I often use speech to express a feeling or an emotion. This was vital to learn about one another. Not to understand this causes many moments of despair.

One evening Jack and I were looking at a full, lovely moon. It was an incredibly beautiful evening, and I said, "Isn't that a beautiful moon?"

What was I really saying? Jack could see the moon. I certainly wasn't pointing it out to him. What I was really saying was this, "This beautiful evening with that full moon makes me feel very romantic!"

When Jack answered, "Yes, it is bright enough to shoot a golf ball by," he grinned very quickly so I knew he was kidding, or I would have dissolved into tears. We had been married long enough by that time for him to pick up my feeling and to respond to it.

If it is raining outside and I look out and say, "Oh, it is raining," I could be expressing a number of things, most of them feelings. I could mean that the rain makes me feel depressed, or it makes me feel energetic, like cleaning house.

If Jack says, "It's raining outside," he is simply saying that the heavens have parted and little drops of moisture are falling to the ground. He is expressing a fact. I am expressing a feeling.

I backed the car out of the garage one day, turning too sharply and taking a piece of the garage along with the fender. I rushed into the house and said, "Oh, I feel just terrible! You can't imagine how awful it was to hear that 'crunch' and . . ."

Jack interrupted, "Never mind that. What happened?"

If that incident had happened a few years before it did, I would have been completely crushed, thinking that Jack was either angry at me, or didn't care whether I was all right or not, or didn't understand. I probably would have cried most of the afternoon. The incident would have triggered that old thought pattern of "he doesn't care how I'm feeling. If he doesn't care about my feelings, he doesn't care about me and he can't love me the way I want to be loved." It could have been days before I got back to the proper perspective.

Instead, I thought, *Oh, yes, he is interested in the facts. He will listen to my feelings later.* And it was all right because I knew he would listen. And he did.

I want to understand. And in that understanding, accept. But I need the wisdom of God to do that. And I need the God of Wisdom. Often I pray, "Lord, help Jack and me fall more in love with each other. Help us understand each other. Help me accept him. Help us become, as a couple, more than we ever could as individuals."

A poem by Roy Croft sums up my feelings:

I love you,
Not only for what you are
But for what I am
When I am with you.

I love you,
Not only for what
You have made of yourself
But for what
You are making of me.
I love you,
For the part of me
That you bring out;
I love you
For putting your hand
Into my heaped-up heart
And passing over
All the foolish, weak things
That you can't help
Dimly seeing there,
And for drawing out
Into the light
All the beautiful belongings
That no one else had looked
Quite far enough to find.
I love you because you
Are helping me to make
Of the lumber of my life
Not a tavern
But a temple;
Out of works
Of my every day
Not a reproach
But a song.[1]

Note
1. Roy Croft, "I Love You," *Best Loved Poems of the American People* (New York: Doubleday, 1936).

CHAPTER SIX

CHOOSING TO CELEBRATE DIFFERENCES

by Jack and Carole

CAROLE

The voice on the other end of the telephone identified herself as the daughter of a long-standing friend. After we chatted for a few minutes, she told me that she and her husband had taken a type-indicator test the night before in preparation for a career change. I could have predicted her next remark. "We are different in everything," she lamented.

"Great!" I replied.

There was a slight gasp on the other end of the phone followed by a long pause. "Do you think being so very different is good?"

"I really do," I responded. "Actually, we've only met a handful of couples who feel they have similar characteristics and responses. And we feel sorry for them."

"Why?" she queried.

"Because they are missing out," I continued. "If they are alike, they may have the same potential strengths, but they'll probably have similar weaknesses, too, which need balance from opposite types of personalities.

"Several months ago, we talked with a couple—married only two years—who were mostly alike. Both were introverts, logical thinkers, plodders, goal-oriented, and organized. As a result, they lacked both social outreach and the ability to have fun together. Neither of them were creative or motivated to spend quality time together on dates and trips—yet they recognized this as a need. They were smart enough to seek out friends who could stimulate them in these weak areas.

"But fortunately, most couples have God-given differences which, if we allow God to use them, help to complete us.

"Then, too, the truth of Proverbs 27:17 is less applicable if we are alike—'Iron sharpens iron, so one man sharpens another.' It's the differences that give the iron its roughness, its sharpening power. Marriage is one of God's best ways to hone us to become more like His Son."

She was silent for a moment. "Um . . . I see what you mean," she said. But I could tell she wasn't convinced that the differences were a positive and not a negative aspect of her marriage.

A wedding day is not a place of arrival, but a place where the adventure begins. A husband and a wife must commit themselves to mutually growing together or we will grow apart. One of the most important needs of growing together is to know who you are and to know—really know—the person you're married to.

Have you ever asked yourself the question, "What would I have to know in order to truly understand who I am? To understand the person I married?"

Here are some areas you would need to explore:

Family background/environment/history/place in family/role models: These factors affect attitudes toward illness, death, gifts, vacations, holidays, work, recreation, culture and the arts, racial issues, sexuality, sharing, showing affection, acceptance, serving, responsibilities.

Spiritual gifts/talents: What creative talents do you or your partner have? Have you been given the gift of mercy, teaching, serving, leadership, hospitality (etc.)? How do these gifts and talents work out in day to day living?

Personal identity in Christ: Head and heart knowledge of this crucial area affects many other areas, such as self-worth, Christ-worth (whether you feel worthless or loved), and struggles to perform versus resting in Christ.

Personality type: Everything from the extrovert/introvert difference to how you process information and come to decisions.

And these are only the beginning! John Fischer comments, "The success of a marriage comes not in finding the 'right' person, but in the ability of both partners to adjust to the real person they inevitably realize they married. Some people never make this adjustment, becoming trapped in the endless search after an image that doesn't exist."[1]

Now let's look briefly at some crucial differences:

The Way We Take in Information.
Some of us take in information by way of the five senses—sight, sound, touch, taste, and smell. Others of us process information by way of a sixth sense—a hunch or, as we usually call it, intuition.

Jack is a "five senses" man, I'm a "sixth sense" woman. Jack identifies with a statement such as, "Most problems precisely defined are already partially solved."[2] But I agree with a statement such as, "A single fact will often spoil an interesting argument."[3]

Jack reads instructions and notices details to process those instructions while I often skip directions and just—try it. In fact, it's become a family joke. When something goes wrong with one of our household appliances and I'm standing there in exasperation, I look at Jack, grin sheepishly and say, "I know. I know. When all else fails, read the instructions."

Jack likes set procedures, established routines, things that are definite and measurable. A practical thinker, he often asks, "Will it work? And if not, why not?" I enjoy change and variety, prefer to imagine possibilities and like opportunities to be inventive and creative. I'll try something to see if it works—and if it doesn't, I don't worry about it. (That's because I can always ask Jack!!)

One clinical psychologist says this difference places the widest gulf of all between people.[4] The way we gather data, influences how we look at life and provides the basis for how we make decisions.

Jack is factual, practical, and thinks sequentially. When looking at a house, Jack looks at the square footage, how the rooms are arranged, the state of the furnace, hot water heater, walls and roof, the conditions of the loan, and financing, and how much upkeep on the house and lawn will be needed.

Not me! To me, the house has to go "Booong" or I won't even look at it twice. When Jack asks what kind of house will go "Booong," I can't tell him—it just has to go "Booong."

But I can see possibilities—and actually my intuitive "Booong" has stood us in good stead over the years.

How We Make Decisions

Once again, we are totally opposite in both how and why we come to a decision. Jack is logical, analytical, objective, cool. He bases his decisions on what is right.

Now, I want to do what is right, too. But in some cases, a higher priority is *how will it affect people*? I lead with my heart, Jack leads with his head. The values of kindness, caring, gentleness, harmony are high on my priority list. Jack wants to be kind and caring (and even gentle), but the principles of truth and justice stand at the top of his priority list.

To be balanced, I desperately need Jack and he greatly needs me! For instance, in any number of cases when Lynn was growing up, I would be too emotionally involved with her to make a good decision. We needed Jack's objective "outside-looking-in" approach to come up with the right thing to do. But left by himself, Jack might not be able to understand how people are feeling about the results of his decision.

The following examples illustrate these differences:

The way we plan.

> I plan when I'm in the mood to think about something.

> Jacks plans based on what needs to be worked on at the moment, whether or not he's in the mood.

In our work habits.

> I just begin without much planning for what needs to be done, or without organizing the work in proper sequence. I see something that needs to be done, and I do it — the fastest and easiest way possible.

> Jack is slower, more careful. He prepares before starting to make sure that he has everything he needs before he begins.

The way we organize.

> I am inclined to do it the easiest, most hassle-free way.

> Jack is inclined to do research, get the facts, and tries to make the best and most logical choice.

The way we play and use leisure time.

> I'm a sightseer, a looker, and want to try new things.

> Jack tends to be a nonparticipant (except in certain sports) and isn't inclined to try new things (but likes it when I talk him into it!).

In our thinking regarding spending time with people.

> I like to spend time with people just for the sake of spending time with people.

> Jack is inclined to review time with people in the light of what has been accomplished.

Life with a total opposite takes a great deal of understanding!
Understand, for instance, that intuitive, feeling people . . .

- ■ may take criticism of their ideas more personally than
  was intended. So take their feelings into account when
  telling them something.
- ■ do not take teasing well — they'll take it personally every
  time!
- ■ tend to over-commit themselves because it's hard for
  them to say no — especially when someone needs help.

Understand, too, that factual, objective people . . .

- ■ need more understanding and support in the emotional
  area because the feeling side of life tends to be less familiar to them.
- ■ will talk more about what they are doing or thinking
  than how they are feeling and may neglect to ask other
  people about how they are feeling.
- ■ may show love more by doing things than by talking
  deeply.
- ■ are often linear learners and will appreciate being led
  through a topic step by step.

Understand, particularly, that the best decisions are those
made *together* by one objective, logical person and one subjective,
feeling person. Those decisions will be thought-through, realistic,
and relevant, but they also will consider the people who will be
affected.

JACK

How can we balance and complement each other when we come
to life with such significant differences?

I can't tell you the specifics of how to do it, because each couple is unique, created by God in different ways. But primary is the need to accept and not try to change the way your partner thinks and responds to life. Secondly, it is necessary to sit down and think of the positive qualities of the way your spouse operates.

Our fun is increased because of Carole's imaginative mind, but the background for those times is well-planned because of the way I think. I assist her to think things through and to set goals. She aids me in relaxing and enjoying life more.

Every couple has to figure out how to maximize their strengths and compensate for each other's weaknesses—and this takes work. So take a weekend, or at least a full day, just for the two of you. Enjoy a wonderful breakfast out and then find a place where you can be alone.

First, pray together about your time, and then separate for an hour. During that hour, pray, read the Word, and talk over with the Lord what your goals should be for the next month, the next six months—maybe even for a year. Make these concrete, measurable goals. (Remember: A goal is something you have control over. A desire is something you'd like to see happen but can't make happen. For instance, you desire that your children be godly. You pray for it. But that can't be a goal because you are not able to control their wills or responses. Your goal might be to teach them a Bible verse each week or to pray for them each day.)

After that hour, get together and share the goals (personal, marriage, family, ministry can all be worked on, but stick to marriage goals for this time), combine them, set some activities that will accomplish those goals along with the scheduled time to do them. Then bring them to the Lord together.

Now, take the rest of the day to enjoy each other!

Any couple who did this every three months or so would make a tremendous beginning toward balancing and completing the way they think.

Over the years we've prayed, "Thank You, Lord, for our diversity. Thank You that we aren't alike. Thank You that You are working in our contrasts to shape us and conform us to Yourself. Thank You that You use these differences to make us see Your world . . . round!"

Pray with us that God will open our eyes to the wonder—the incredible phenomenon—of being one even as we are different. Of having unity even in our diversity.

To review:

- Listen with your heart.
- Communicate until you understand.
- Grow in understanding until you accept.
- Continue accepting until you can affirm.
- Affirm until you can grow in the strengths of the other.
- Periodically set goals for your marriage and review them.

And may one of the topics, for both goal-setting and communication, be the question, "How can we begin to work on using our differences to be assets in our marriage rather than liabilities? What practical things can we do to make them possibilities rather than problems?"

Difficult? You bet!

Exciting? Definitely.

And, my friends, time worth spending.

Now—just do it!

Notes

1. John Fisher, "The Image," *Partnership* (January-February 1988).
2. Harry Lorayne, quoted in "Quotable Quotes," *Reader's Digest* (November 1988), p. 33.
3. From *Selected Cryptograms III*, quoted in "Quotable Quotes," p. 33.
4. David Keirsey and Marilyn Bates, *Please Understand Me* (Del Mar, Calif.: Prometheus Nemesis Books, 1978), p. 17.

CHAPTER SEVEN

CHOOSING TO ADJUST

by Jack

Scripts. That's the difficulty.

"When two actors go out on stage, we take it for granted that they both are going to be working from the same script," writes Dr. Carlfred Broderick. "By the same token, when two people marry they put down their five dollars in a similar hope that they can take a particular script for granted. Unfortunately, the scripts from which each member of a couple plays her and his marital scenes are sometimes very different . . . Often our scripts are based on our parents' marriages."[1]

Dr. Broderick tells of a man from a family of five with strict rules for sharing their two bathrooms. When the door was shut, no one would think even of knocking, let alone entering.

The young man married a woman from a family of five people with only one bathroom, and everyone had walked in and out of that one bathroom at will. So of course she never gave a thought to walking in on her husband in their bathroom. He, however, was so taken aback that he couldn't speak!

Then Dr. Broderick gives an example from his own marriage:

In the early days of my own marriage I would have sworn that my wife and I had discussed every aspect of life and love. We had known each other from kindergarten, dated from the tenth grade and been engaged for a year and a half. But we never discussed what happens when you are sick. And if someone had suggested we discuss it, I would have laughed.

Every right-thinking person knows what you should do when you get sick—you go to bed. That is your part. Then your mother, or whoever loves you, pumps you full of fruit juice.

Well, I married this woman I had known all my life, and in the natural course of events I caught the flu. I knew what to do, of course. I went to bed and waited. But nothing happened. Nothing. I couldn't believe it!

I was so hurt, I would have left if I hadn't been so ill. Finally I asked about juice and she brought me some—in a little four-ounce glass. Period. Because as I learned later, the only time they drank juice at her house was on alternate Tuesdays, when they graced breakfast with a drop in a thimble-sized glass. My family's "juice glasses" held twelve ounces and there was always someone standing by to refill them.[2]

The success of a marriage may hinge on whether we allow such trivial things to irritate, annoy, and drive us apart or whether we work to understand, accept and adjust to one another.

Carole and I came to marriage thinking we really were approaching this drama from the same script. After all, both of us were raised in Christian homes and in middle-class neighborhoods; our parents had good marriages, loved their children, were firm but not strict disciplinarians; we attended the same college, had some of the same friends, and had gone together for three and a half years when we walked down the aisle.

So it came with some surprise when we realized that not only were we reading from unrelated scripts, but at times we didn't even seem to be on the same stage.

We ran into the two-stage problem our very first Christmas. Carole wanted to wait until Christmas morning to open gifts! Can you believe that? Every sane person knows that Christmas Eve is the time to gather around the tree and open gifts. But no. Christmas Eve, said Carole, was the time to have the Christmas story and sing carols. And then early Christmas morning, one woke in excited anticipation of stockings filled with goodies. After a hurried breakfast, the gifts would be opened one by one with each taking a turn giving out a gift to another. It took her family hours, and Christmas dinner was forgotten in the process. Imagine that! No traditional Christmas dinner.

And Christmas wasn't the only holiday we celebrated in divergent ways. There was Valentine's Day (she celebrated it, I didn't); Easter (a new outfit was essential but she had to wear it Palm Sunday so she wouldn't think about the new clothes on Easter; I can never remember having a new outfit); and the Fourth of July (big family reunion for Carole; fireworks in the park for me).

But at least you could say our stages were in the same theater. And over the years Carole and I have grown together. We now celebrate Christmas both on Christmas Eve, with the Christmas story and carols and half our gifts — given slowly one by one — and on Christmas morning, with the rest of our gifts and a traditional Christmas dinner to boot. We've joined our traditions to make a year rich with celebrations.

But in reality, how special days are celebrated is one of the easy ones.

Scripts are especially difficult to handle in the area of ethnic differences.

We have friends who, four years into their marriage, knew they had a giant problem. She was a reserved German, he a volatile

Italian. Whenever they disagreed, he raised his voice and shouted. She withdrew.

It seemed to her that he was always shouting whether they were disagreeing or not. And she withdrew even further.

When they went to a counselor, he suggested that they take ten minutes to talk before the children were up. He gave them specific instructions on how to spend those ten minutes. She could talk on any topic she wished to and he was not to say a word. The next morning he could answer her. This gave him twenty-four hours to think about his response and be more controlled in his tone of voice. Then he could introduce another subject or add to the one she had initiated. She could not respond until the third morning.

It took them several months to work through the backlog of things she'd been repressing, but today they have one of the most beautiful marriages you'd want to see.

Because the scripts we use are so different, understanding family background is imperative. In "Discussion Questions for Better Communication" (beginning on page 247), we've listed areas to talk about relating to family background. If you've never done it before, you might want to take an hour or two each week to explore these questions.

Someone has said, "A successful marriage requires falling in love many times, always with the same person."[3]

That's true. Part of the process of falling in love—and staying in love—demands a knowledge and understanding of the background of our partner. This awareness comes through hard work, communication, compromise, adjusting. And a giant helping of God's grace.

Notes
1. Carlfred Broderick, "How to Rewrite Your Marriage Script So It Works," *Redbook* (February 1979), p. 21.
2. Broderick.
3. Mignon McLaughlin in *The Atlantic*, quoted in "Quotable Quotes," *Reader's Digest* (July 1989), p. 8.

PART THREE
COMMUNICATION

CHAPTER EIGHT

CHOOSING TO COMPREHEND:
INTROVERT/EXTROVERT

by Jack

As the wedding processional ended, the ushers began dismissing the guests by rows. We stood to go through the reception line when I leaned close to Carole and whispered, "Let's skip the reception."

She grinned and said, "Maybe we'll be able to duck out after thirty minutes or so."

Years ago this little exchange would have ended up in a major conflict. Carole would have either (1) groaned at my suggestion (2) decided that I was an unsociable lout, (3) agreed to skip the reception but felt cheated the rest of the day or (4) insisted on staying while feeling put out that I'd even suggested leaving.

Today we understand each other better.

Carole now knows I'm not necessarily unsociable and I don't hate people. But I *am* an introvert. And the battery of an introvert gets drained at wedding receptions. If I'm low on energy to begin with, a wedding reception has the appeal of a swamp full of water-snakes.

Introverts get bad press in the United States. When one hears the word "introvert," a picture comes to mind of a person who doesn't like to be with people, who is solitary, reclusive, unsociable and silent. Of most introverts, not true!

A few years ago, Carole and I came across a definition of an introvert and extrovert which helped us understand each other in a new way. An introvert is simply a person who is energized—or draws strength—from internal sources and experience. He or she is one who reflects—and then (maybe) acts.

An extrovert, on the other hand, is one who is energized or draws strength from external sources—from other people and external experiences; one who acts, then (maybe) reflects.[1]

Now it is true that an introvert is often reserved, quiet, and perhaps difficult to know. They need privacy and time alone, and some could seem withdrawn to extroverts. But one of their great contributions is that they give life depth. They think before they speak. They reflect and contemplate, becoming the poets, the philosophers, the theologians.

The extrovert, on the other hand, may be talkative, friendly, easy to know, and may express emotions readily. They need relationships to a greater extent than the introvert. Extroverts give breadth to life.

Now most extroverts want and need time alone. Many introverts want and need time with people. But introverts require more time by themselves in order to draw on their internal resources. To misunderstand this critical difference can cause conflict and distress in a marriage.

The older we become, the closer Carole and I grow on this one. Carole values solitude more in these years of our lives and I have developed a greater capacity for people in social and ministry situations. However, Carole can still be with people longer without getting exhausted than I can which we now take into consideration when we plan a trip. And she appreciates my reminding her when she says "yes" to too many things and begins to go on sheer determination, setting herself up for collapse.

The way an extrovert and introvert think differs as well. A great many extroverts think out loud because hearing themselves say things to other people helps them to better clarify their own understanding. An introvert, however, often keeps his thinking process inside — reflecting, weighing, considering — and only when a conclusion has been reached is he ready to share his thoughts out loud with others.

Introverts get nervous when extroverts think out loud as the introvert may interpret what is being said as a conclusion. Extroverts may feel threatened when an introvert thinks in isolation and feels put out that their opinions aren't being considered.

This difference needs to be met head-on, understood, and then *appreciated*. But, boy, it took us a while.

Much of life is affected by these tendencies.

Vacations. Typical are our friends. Her ideal vacation is a big, luxury hotel in a populated resort area. But her husband wants to camp on a small island and hike, preferably in the rain! She loves tours, he longs for a solitary drive. She wants to visit family and friends, he wants to back-pack in the mountains.

Vacations to an extrovert are often filled with activity and people. To an introvert, vacations mean getting away from it all.

Entertaining and social gatherings. Being the introvert, I tend to want to relate to a few (one to four) deeply rather than many casually so I'll single out one person and have an in-depth discussion rather than go from group to group. Carole, the extrovert, loves — or at least doesn't mind — the big dinner parties, potluck suppers at the church, and various kinds of people get-togethers. Carole relates deeply to a few friends but at a big gathering, she doesn't want to miss anyone! We've discovered that her capacity to keep "up" after days of ministering or relating with people is greater than mine because certain people energize her while even the most interesting ones drain my batteries after a while.

Number of friends and acquaintances. Extroverts usually have a greater number of people with whom they want to stay in touch but introverts will often have significantly more depth in their (fewer) relationships.

We kind of smile at one of our extrovert friends as he describes someone as "a close friend." Being acquainted with the "close friend" he is describing, we know from that friend's viewpoint, it is only an acquaintance. But to our extrovert friend, no one is "just an acquaintance."

The name of the extrovert/introvert game is *compromise*. How? Perhaps by going to the party—but only staying a limited time; by taking work to do so the other can get needed time alone on a trip; by maintaining separate relationships that don't involve the other; by giving each other space to think out loud or in isolation, to talk or not to talk, to relate or not to relate.

Above all, the extrovert and introvert personalities must be understood and accepted—in order to love. In order to grow in marriage.

In order to be—as you desire to be—*best friends*.

Note
1. Earle C. Page, *Looking at Types* (Gainesville, Fla.: C.A.P.T., 1983).

CHAPTER NINE

CHOOSING TO ANALYZE:
PERFECTIONIST/NON-PERFECTIONIST

by Jack and Carole

JACK

We pulled up in front of the small repair garage and parked our rental car. The lock on the back door of this station wagon was jammed and for two days, I'd had to climb over the back seat for suitcases and golf clubs. So here we were at a garage recommended by our hotel manager, impatient to continue our week-long holiday in Scotland on this beautiful day.

After finding out that the repairs would take about half an hour, Carole wandered across the street to explore the ruins of a beautiful old abbey.

When she came back, the door was fixed and I was busy straightening out the mess in the rear of the car. She looked at what I was doing and asked, "Why don't you leave that till later?"

Irritated at her "why" question, I replied firmly, "Because I want to straighten it out now."

"Well, don't get mad at me."

"Well, you always argue with me," I said defensively.

Now at this time, Carole and I had been married thirty-five years! In fact, that trip was a celebration of our thirty-fifth anniversary. Yet in just four sentences, we violated three rules of good relationships. (You have to work hard to do that!)

First, Carole asked a threatening "why" question. Second, I used the inflammatory "always"—unwise at best, and obviously not true. Few of us human beings are consistent enough for "always" and "never" to describe our actions. Third, we had failed (again) to understand how different we are.

For the next ten minutes in the car, things were extremely quiet. Then Carole began to chuckle and so did I. We were laughing at ourselves and the dumb stunt we'd just pulled. We apologized to each other, talked it through, and proceeded to have a wonderful day.

Fifteen or twenty years before, it probably would have taken us the whole day to resolve the conflict arising from that four-sentence exchange. But God has taught us some things in the intervening years—about being open in sharing our feelings quickly, not sulking, and forgiving quickly. But another important factor we have discovered is not to stop with forgiving, but to use the conflict to learn about ourselves and each other.

What had happened here? What was the core reason for our squabble? As we talked, we realized that the fundamental cause of the heated dispute hinged on the reason I was carefully straightening out the suitcases and golf clubs.

The fact of the matter is that I tend to be a perfectionist, and Carole is not. I wouldn't call Carole sloppy; but Carole is, well, fast.

From my point of view, the logical, necessary thing to do after the back door of the station wagon was fixed was to get the mess cleaned up—in an orderly fashion.

But what did Carole want to do when she came back from her exploration of the abbey? Why, she wanted to get going, of course. We'd already wasted half an hour, and all of Scotland lay before us!

Now we knew this characteristic about each other; we just forgot it for a moment and so didn't apply our understanding to that particular situation—or we would have been more considerate and accepting on that lovely morning.

When Carole and I first got married, we were one hundred and eighty degrees apart on this one. But over the years, we've adjusted and changed and now we are apart, oh, maybe twenty degrees or so. That may be all the progress we're going to make in this lifetime. But still, that's a lot of progress!

Of course, there are still some things we don't do together because of this difference. For instance, we don't wash a car together.

Can you picture that? Carole has her bucket and sponge and I have my bucket and sponge and we begin on each side of the car. Whish, whish, whish and three minutes later Carole says "I'm finished" while I'm still working on the front fender. I look up in amazement and go around to inspect her side. Then I make some dumb statement like, "You call that finished?" (It's a wonder I haven't gotten a bucket of water over my head!)

We don't hang wallpaper together. I insist on the lines being straight up and down. Enough said on that one.

A perfectionist, it's said, takes great pains and gives them to everyone else. And I must admit, I now feel sorry for those who have to live with a rigid and extreme perfectionist.

CAROLE

Perfectionists mystify me. Non-perfectionists just stand and shake their heads in disbelief at some things perfectionists do. Things like:

- using two napkins for meals—a cloth one for their lap and a paper one to wipe their hands on.
- keeping separate dish towels for glassware, dishes, pans.
- hanging shirts or blouses by sleeve length, color coordinated, facing forward, hangers all in one direction.

Now I admire many things about a perfectionist. I know one lady who is past her ninetieth birthday but still looks at all times as though she just stepped out of a fashion magazine. Even her robe and slippers match. She spends time searching for the precise shade of earrings, shoes, purse, or blouse to create the perfect combination. I admire that greatly. (And sometimes I even work on it!) But it is simply not a big priority for me. My purse and shoes rarely match because I stay with one neutral-color purse. It simply takes too much time to change purses for every outfit. If my shoes and jewelry go with my suit, it's only because it was just as fast to put on the matching ones.

I can clean my house in two and a half hours (now you know I can't move the furniture in that amount of time, or wash windows). I can fix dinner in twenty minutes, wash the car in fifteen— or less. I go for the fastest, easiest way to do things. So I don't hang my clothes out on the line to air-freshen them. I don't iron anything I don't have to, and my garden takes minimum upkeep.

Of course, as in every characteristic we've talked about, great inconsistencies abound. If a picture is crooked, I have to straighten it (if I have time). The chrome on the kitchen sink may need shining, but the counter must be wiped clean (if I have time). The dining room table needs refinishing and is ignored (I don't have time!). However, it bothers me if the towels in the bathroom aren't folded twice and precisely centered (and I make time!).

Inconsistent? Yes. But as one sage observed, the only consistent thing in this world is that we are inconsistent.

Behold Jack, the perfectionist, who wants a picture light placed in such a way that the cord goes into the wall and not down the outside even if it means a major electrical job. The overhead fan must be exactly centered, the wallpaper perfectly hung. His undershirts are meticulously folded and stacked neatly in the drawer.

But his desk is cluttered (and I don't dare touch it because he knows exactly where things are) and his tools in the basement haven't been organized for years.

Perhaps the secret is not only to understand in general our various traits and characteristics, but also to know thoroughly our particular exceptions and those of our marriage partner.

We probably also need to know the drawbacks of being quick-and-easy versus perfectionistic. For me, one of the major liabilities of being a fast person is that I want things done right now and I want others to be ready to do and go right now too.

I remember well, though it happened years ago, an episode while we were on a trip with Jack's parents to the New York World's Fair. Mom Mayhall, who is an absolute dear but a perfectionist, usually had one more thing to do when my schedule said we were to leave for the day. So I began "managing" (a nice term for nagging), making suggestions to all concerned such as, "Don't forget, we leave at eight o'clock." . . . "You will be ready at eight, won't you?" . . . and finally, "MOM, are you ready to leave?"

One night Jack told me in no uncertain terms to "stop it!" And I hadn't even realized I was doing it!

I was crushed. I also felt helpless as I realized this characteristic of bossiness, brought on by being so "fast," had become an ingrained habit I was unaware of. I cried and prayed all night. I felt that even though Jack had to love me (he was my husband, right?), he probably didn't like me.

It took me three days of saying scarcely anything for fear I'd say the wrong thing, to finally get God's perspective on it. I begged God to change me, but realized that I needed Him first to make me aware of what I was doing and then to change me from the inside. Not just my deliberate actions, though I needed to change them too, but my inner gentleness.

God is not finished with me yet on this one. And it helped to realize that it wasn't a matter of Jack's not liking me. He was really trying to help me in this thing.

Sometimes we can even laugh over this difference now.

I loved this story I read recently: A couple was discussing the wallpaper they had just hung. Don was annoyed at Debby's indifference to what he felt was a poor job. "The problem is that I'm a perfectionist and you're not," he finally said to her.

"Exactly!" she replied enthusiastically. "That's why you married me and I married you!"[1]

JACK

Perfectionists just stand and shake their heads in disbelief at some things that non-perfectionists do:

- Rush through tasks so fast they have to be done over again — and sometimes again, and again.
- Drop things, spill things, break things because they're in such a hurry.
- Settle for just getting things done rather than getting them done right (whether it is washing a car, hanging wallpaper, or weeding the garden).

Words describing a perfectionist are: correct, precise, orderly, neat, careful. They want to *do it right*.

A non-perfectionist uses phrases such as: "let's go!"; "never mind"; "it's okay"; "don't worry." They want to *do it now*.

My mother gave us a colorful windsock one Christmas. Because it was a bit too long for one part of the patio, we temporarily put it away. Then the next summer when Mom was coming for a visit, I saw Carole out on the patio reaching up as far as she could at the edge of the deck to hammer a nail onto a beam. Soon the windsock was blowing gently in the wind.

The next morning the windsock was lying on the deck. It had blown off the nail, of course, in a stronger wind that night.

Still in my pajamas, I got an enclosed bracket, a ladder, measured the exact place the sock should hang, and put it up the right way. But to my critical eye, I thought the sock was a bit long even for that part of the patio. (Perfectionists tend to be critical, did you know that?)

But I guess if Carole hadn't hung it wrong, I wouldn't have hung it right! Fortunately, God knew what He was doing when

He chose Carole and me for each other. If I had married my own type, would anything ever get done? And if Carole had married her own type, would anything get done well? I'm so grateful He led us together.

How to Complete, Not Compete

How important it is to look at the positives in this particular difference. If you don't, you may go a little nuts!

I admit there have been times when I've been irritated because of missing socks, pink shorts (because something red got mixed in with the white wash), collars that wouldn't lie right because of being pressed hurriedly. But what a bonus it is that I rarely have to wait for Carole! She is usually ready to go before I am. She entertains easily because she isn't insistent that the house or the meal be perfect. She isn't an uptight person and accepts herself and others readily. Friends, those are things to be thankful for.

On the other hand, Carole appreciates the fact that I do things carefully. She rarely needs to get involved in our travel plans—and we travel almost half of the time. She knows I'll carefully investigate the best prices for rental cars, hotels, and get the needed receipts. I keep the books, including balancing the checkbook. And I've even learned to be patient (most of the time) when Carole copies the amount of the check incorrectly or subtracts the amount wrong and so the balance is a few cents off at the end of the month. She tries. She just does it so quickly that she sometimes makes mistakes.

But aren't you glad that some people are perfectionists? How would you like a non-perfectionist dentist, doctor, engineer, or tailor? And aren't you glad there are fast people? Think of perfectionistic artists who would never be satisfied with what they wrote or painted—and so they'd keep their art to themselves rather than let others enjoy it. Or perfectionistic people managers, who would demand so much of their team that "good" would never be "good enough."

It is critical that we allow the sharpening process in one another's lives to take place in this area. I'm much easier to work for and live with, and much more accepting of myself and others, because I've lived with Carole all these years. And she has slowed down in some things, taking time to do them right the first time. She has learned to organize, set priorities, and select the important over the inconsequential much more often than when we first married.

We need each other.

We learn from each other.

And I kid you not, it's fun to be married to each other. Honestly, the delight is not only in the ways we are alike, but in the differences as well.

Note
1. "Life in These United States," by B.N.M. of Chicago, *Reader's Digest* (May 1988), p. 113.

CHAPTER TEN

CHOOSING TO ASSESS:
AGGRESSIVE/TIMID

by Jack and Carole

JACK

The steak house came highly recommended. After we eased into a booth, I placed our order confidently: "We'll have the filets — medium, please."

Fifteen minutes later, the waiter placed our steaks before us. I could see the blood running even before I took an investigative cut. "This steak is too rare," I declared.

"Sweetheart," Carole murmured, "why don't you trade with me? I don't mind it cooked that way."

"Yes, you do," I countered and glanced at her plate. "And anyway, yours is rare too." I raised my hand in a futile attempt to attract the waiter's attention.

"Let's not make a fuss," Carole begged. "Can't we just ignore it and enjoy the evening?"

"Hey, we're paying good money for this steak. I'm going to send them both back," I insisted and succeeded this time in summoning our waiter.

We waited another fifteen minutes before our steaks appeared again. As I cut into them, I groaned. "Oh, no, now they're cooked to death! No way are they medium."

Carole chided, "Well, they were probably upset that you sent them back."

"That's their problem," I retorted.

Once again I called the waiter as Carole tried to disappear under the tablecloth. And finally our steaks were served — medium. But I don't think Carole enjoyed hers very much.

I'm sure most of you have either participated in or witnessed such a scenario. And you've either cheered or been embarrassed by it, depending upon your nature.

The characteristic of assertiveness is called by many names. If you and I are both assertive, I might call you hostile; but me? Well, I'm forceful. I'll name you belligerent; me, enterprising. The other person is pugnacious, but I'm energetic. That one is contentious, but I am zealous. (Would you believe that all of these are synonyms of the word "assertive" in my thesaurus?)

Sometimes this characteristic leads to embarrassing conclusions. This story appeared in *The Vail Trail's Pastimes*:

> Dan Mulrooney, owner of Bart and Yeti's, tells the story of an impatient patron who, seeing that all the tables were filled and after being told that there would be an hour wait, demanded to see Bart. "I'm a close personal friend of Bart's and I want to see him. He'll get me a table."
>
> The bar, of course, was named after two dogs.
>
> So Mulrooney said, "You're a close personal friend of his, huh?"
>
> The would-be patron insisted he was.
>
> "He's kind of busy," Mulrooney said, "but since you're such a close friend of his, I'll get him."
>
> Leading the dog to the hostess stand, Mulrooney said, "This is Bart, see if he can get you a table."
>
> The man decided against dinner at Bart and Yeti's.[1]

So much for assertiveness!

On the other hand, if I am the opposite of assertive, I may call timidity a number of things as well. I may say you're fainthearted, but I'm humble. I call him fearful; myself, retiring. She is wishy-washy; I'm a peacemaker.

The many names for assertiveness and timidity indicate the many and varied aspects of these traits. Obviously, there are both negative and positive sides to each.

The positive side of forceful people's character is that they take charge when necessary and are usually outspoken on behalf of others as well as themselves.

The negative counterpart may be that they tend to be rigid, very control-oriented, and perhaps belligerent. They can also be overly independent to the point of not asking for help—such as being lost but not stopping to ask directions. More serious is that many people who have this characteristic hesitate to go for counseling until a major disaster or crisis has already occurred.

The positive side of compliant people is that they tend to be peacemakers, polite, and easy on others or themselves. On the negative side, they may be indecisive, and in their desire not to ruffle anyone's feathers, they can act out of weakness rather than on firm convictions.

At first glance, this difference doesn't seem to be a big deal. But it can be! When the self-assured partner overwhelms and rides over the timid one, when daily situations cause embarrassment or loss of respect, or when either tendency is carried to an extreme, then it can loom large in a relationship.

CAROLE

I'm sure there are people who need "assertiveness training." I probably need to take a course in it one of these days. I'm the kind of person who doesn't like to return things to a store (I'd sooner be out the money); I'll wriggle out of making unpleasant phone calls if I possibly can; I'd rarely ask for a different table at a restaurant or return food not cooked well; I'd rather wipe dirty silverware with my napkin than ask the waitress for replacements; I won't speak to a smoker in a non-smoking section (though I'm getting better at this one). If someone shouts at me, I'm inclined to withdraw or cry — rather than speak back firmly (I'd rarely shout back). I'm not sure if my peace-at-any-price attitude is based on fear or on wanting to keep the situation as calm and peaceful as possible.

Regardless of motive, to me the enjoyment of time together is much more important than how my eggs are cooked. If rectifying a situation is necessary, then I want it done quietly and pleasantly, without threat to the pleasure of companionship.

Assertiveness often turns into negative aggressiveness. I've seen people, in the name of standing up for rights, get belligerent, impolite, and unkind. Perhaps assertiveness training should be followed up by a course on manners. Nevertheless, if I didn't have Jack, I would need Assertiveness Training 101 because it is often exactly the trait needed in some situations.

Perhaps a naturally forceful person has the potential for leading. Or it could be he is a born "thinker" and comes up with ideas along with the drive to put them into practice. Whatever is involved, I'm glad I married a person who is always thinking and isn't afraid to speak up about his good ideas. On one occasion in particular I had opportunity to be very grateful for Jack's refusal to back off when events didn't turn out the way we'd expected.

Our daughter and her husband were in language school in Costa Rica, and we were making a trip to visit them. We had been speaking at a conference center in Tennessee, and so our flight plan was Chattanooga-Atlanta, Atlanta-Miami, and Miami-Costa Rica, then returning through Venezuela to visit missionaries there. We had saved a great deal of money by purchasing an advance ticket that could not be changed in any way.

The night before our departure, we had dinner in Chattanooga with friends, told the clerk at our motel near the airport we would need a ride to the terminal at 6:45 a.m. for an 8:00 a.m. flight, and retired early. (Of course, I kept waking up to check the time and make sure we would hear the alarm.)

We arrived with our luggage at the front desk next morning at 6:45. The same clerk who had been on duty the night before said, "You're running a bit late, aren't you?" to which we replied, "Why, no. It's six-forty-five."

She replied, "No, it's seven-forty-five!"

We were horrified to discover that seven miles out of Chattanooga, the time zone changed! Not once during dinner or at the motel had we seen a clock with local time.

We made a mad dash to the airport but were greeted with the sight of our plane taking off. We had missed the first lap of our trip to Costa Rica with no apparent way to catch up to our Atlanta-Miami flight.

I was sick at heart and sick to my stomach!

But my dear husband is always thinking. A car rental was out—the drive was too long to make our flight out of Atlanta. To break into our "excursion ticket" would have cost about five hundred dollars each—a thousand dollars we didn't have. As we prayed, Jack asked the airline ticket agent, "What about chartering a plane to Atlanta?" The agent's face lit up as he said, "It would cost you one hundred and sixty dollars, but that's certainly less than a new ticket."

In twenty minutes we were at a small hanger, our luggage stowed in a plane all ready to take off. But the pilot didn't show up! We waited for him until it was too late to catch our next lap in Atlanta. I was fighting tears. But Jack's mind kept buzzing as he prayed and I worried (I knew even then that what he did was more effective).

When the pilot finally came, our only alternative seemed to be to cancel everything and wait until the next day. However, not only would that have cost us the thousand dollars, but we had no way to contact our loved ones who were waiting in Costa Rica.

Jack kept thinking. He discovered another flight that could make our Miami-Costa Rica connection, and off we went in a little four-seater to Atlanta. A shuttle-bus whisked us to the gate fifteen minutes before departure.

But when the agent at the counter looked at our tickets, she said, "I can't let you on this plane without rewriting your whole ticket, and I don't have time to do that before the plane leaves."

My heart seemed to drop right through the floor.

Jack's assertiveness came to the fore. "Lady," he said firmly, "you've got to get us on that plane. There must be a way you can help us." She hesitated and then said, "Well, I could let you go on standby and then we wouldn't have to rewrite your ticket."

The plane had plenty of room, so we went standby and finally caught up with our originally planned flight in Miami. I didn't take a relaxed breath, however, until we were on the Miami-Costa Rica lap of the trip. Then I thanked God fervently for working things out and for my ever-thinking assertive husband. And I felt sorry for all the couples in the world who are both nonassertive. I guess in those cases, one would have to pray and work extra-hard at learning to keep thinking, to keep pressing, to keep insisting.

Perhaps nonassertive people are more likely to be worriers. Even though I am by nature optimistic, sometimes negative ideas and thoughts plague me: "We're late, so they probably won't hold our reservations"; "What if we get lost? We'll never find our way back"; "We need to leave a detailed itinerary in case something happens."

Part of that, I suppose, is my mind for the details along with my concern for the "what ifs" of life. But part of it may be that I tend to feel the situation controls me instead of my having the ability to control the situation.

Now I have learned to force myself to do things I might not be inclined to do. I can confront if I have to. In fact, sometimes in my need for unclouded relationships, I confront when Jack might want to let it go—not if it has to do with the two of us, but sometimes with other people.

So in situations involving interpersonal relationships, I may be the assertive one. In almost all other situations, Jack takes that responsibility—and much more naturally than I do. In all honesty, I depend on him to take charge aggressively when I'm either at a total loss for words or just naturally reticent.

I need him. He needs me.

The aggressive individual needs the caution of the peacemaker. The timid needs the bold. The forceful "I'm going to win" person needs another to warn him about breaking relationships and to remind him of the importance of understanding over winning. Yet the peace-at-any-price personality needs the confronter to emphasize that she can't resolve issues by avoiding them.

JACK

But supposing the wife is the aggressive one and the man is the non-confronter—an even more difficult scenario to be worked through. Wives who feel a man would rather switch than fight may see that as lack of leadership. A husband who has a wife who is aggressive or even outgoing may think she isn't the biblical wife of 1 Peter 3:4 (NIV), which says, "Instead, it [your beauty] should be that of your inner self, the unfading beauty of a gentle and quiet spirit, which is of great worth in God's sight."

I've met men who equate "quiet spirit" with "quiet personality." They couldn't be more wrong!

A quiet spirit has to do with a person's inner spiritual life. A person who is humble, dependent on God and looking to Him moment by moment, *has* a quiet spirit no matter what her personality type. A husband has the responsibility to help his wife become a woman of God, but in no way should he (or can he!) change her personality.

Even as men sometimes equate a quiet spirit with a quiet personality, women tend to equate aggressiveness with leadership. If a husband has the gift of mercy and is a non-confronter and peacemaker by nature, a wife may not see him as a leader. Wrong, again!

Leadership does not depend upon personality. Leadership is about assuming responsibility. But we'll get to this in a later chapter.

Solomon puts it this way, "Iron sharpens iron, so one man sharpens another" (Proverbs 27:17). In a real sense, God can take a husband and wife and use them to polish and hone each other into diamonds that will better reflect Jesus Christ.

Four steps of action need to be taken to defuse any potentially explosive situation:

1. Know your mate—study her or him so that you get to know her or him well.
2. Understand your mate—this has to do with communication. Get things out in the open and talk about them. It also needs prayer—asking God for the wisdom to understand the person to whom you are married.
3. Adjust to your mate—this has to do with a willingness and openness on your part to change and adjust together so that you truly *do* fit together.
4. Accept your mate—this is an important aspect of love.

Know, understand, adjust, and accept. These are choices we have to make.

And remember, God created us both.

May our differences, then, become unbreakable links forged by God Himself, hammered out on the anvil of the everydayness of living . . . and loving.

Together.

Note
1. Quoted from *The Vail Trail's Pastimes* (August 26, 1988), p. 12.

CHAPTER ELEVEN

CHOOSING TO CLARIFY

by Carole

I am constantly amazed at the insights of Charles Schulz in his
Peanuts cartoon strip. One Sunday I both laughed and sighed
at the frustration of poor Charlie Brown as I read the following:

PEPPERMINT PATTY: Explain love to me, Chuck.
CHARLIE BROWN: You can't explain love . . . I can recommend a book, or a painting, or a song, or a poem, but I
can't explain love.
PP: Try, Chuck! Try to explain love . . .
CB: Well, say I happen to see this cute little girl walk by,
and I . . .
PP: Why does she have to be cute, Chuck? Can't someone
fall in love with a girl who isn't cute, and has freckles and
a big nose? Explain that Chuck! !
CB: Well, maybe you're right. . . . Let's just say, then, that I
happen to see this girl walk by who has a great big nose,
and . . .
PP (yelling): I didn't say a great big nose, Chuck!
CB (flat on his back): You not only can't explain love . . .
actually, you can't even talk about it. . . .[1]

Charlie Brown had difficulty communicating on a complex topic like love. For many of us, even talking about ordinary subjects seems unattainable.

However, we cannot expect the wages of happiness if we do not work for them. Communication—the right kind of communication—is probably the most vital ingredient in the success of our marriages. Love cannot exist without it.

J. A. Fritze, a Lutheran minister and clinical counselor, has said, "You can't know anyone unless you communicate with them. You can't love anything you don't know. Therefore, the depth of love existing between a husband and wife will largely depend on the amount and depth of their communication."[2]

A simple definition of communication is that it is "a process, (either verbal or non-verbal) of sharing information with another person in such a way that he understands what you are saying."[3] The key word is *understanding*.

In the last few years, Jack and I have learned a great deal about clarifying meaning . . . hard work for me. I am adept at circling issues, going off into tangents to try to make a point, coding my messages and hoping Jack can decode them. My goal is consistently to "say what I mean and mean what I say" and, though I seldom reach this goal, I know that "If you aim at nothing, you are bound to hit it."

Remember, it is more important to think together than to think alike. Jack and I will never think alike, and that's fine. To bring two different ways of thinking together adds perspective and strength to our marriage. We have to learn to bring our wavelengths together constantly so that we are continually understanding one another. The most helpful way that we have found to do this is by asking questions such as, "What do you mean?" "What are you really saying?" "This is how I'm taking what you have just said," and rephrasing the statement. We have been amazed that even after many years of living together, we still misunderstand the other's meaning unless we clarify often in this way.

Communication specialists tell us that there are six messages involved in the communication process:

1. What you mean to say.
2. What you actually say.
3. What the other person hears.
4. What the other person thinks he hears.
5. What the other person says about what you said.
6. What you think the other person said about what you said.[4]

Gets a bit complicated, doesn't it?

In chapter 5, I mentioned an incident when Jack and I were looking at a gorgeous moon together under romantic circumstances. As we shared that moment, how was I actually feeling? I was feeling romantic. If we followed the six messages, that incident would have looked something like this:

1. What you mean to say. "The moon puts me in a romantic mood."
2. What you actually say. "Isn't that a brilliant moon?"
3. What the other person hears. "The moon is bright."
4. What the other person thinks he hears. "The moon is bright enough for a walk."
5. What the other person says about what you said. "Yes, it's bright enough to shoot a golf ball by."
6. What you think the other person said about what you said. "I don't feel romantic."

We can miss each other's wavelengths completely by the time the six messages are completed without even realizing what has happened. All of us are constantly in the process of coding and decoding messages. We can't avoid this, though it is something we must work on. For instance, Jack may come home from work and ask a simple question, such as, "When is dinner?"

I could interpret his question as, "I'm very hungry. Could you hurry dinner so we can eat right away?"

I would be entirely wrong. Jack likes to walk before dinner several times a week. So what he could be asking is, "Do I have time to exercise before dinner, or are you cooking something that can't wait?"

Because we have been working on "saying what we mean," he is more frequently asking, "Do I have time to walk before dinner?" which is not a coded message. But when he doesn't clarify, I need to say, "Do you want to exercise before dinner or are you especially hungry and want me to hurry it up?"

Being much more logical and factual than I am, Jack doesn't send as many ambiguous messages as I do. And he is getting adept at decoding my confusing messages. But now when I hear myself sending a complicated verbal thought, I am more likely to catch myself and state it more clearly. I'll say, "I guess what I am really trying to say . . ." and clarify. But because I am the kind of person I am, I know I'll never do this perfectly, nor will any of us for that matter. So we need to learn to ask questions, or restate the point for clarification of meaning.

On a visit to England, we had a delightful day with some friends. Driving along the freeway, Jeannie suddenly said, "It's five o'clock." Now all of us had watches. We were aware of the time. Obviously that statement held more than was on the surface. We laughed and said, "Okay, Jeannie, what are you really saying?"

What she was really saying was, "Do I have time to go home and check on the children before we go out for dinner?" But I wonder if we hadn't asked her to clarify, would she have gone through that entire evening worrying about her children and frustrated because we had failed to pick up her meaning?

We are proficient at dropping small coded gems into our conversations. If someone doesn't pick up the signals, we may be wounded without that person even being aware of our hurt. It is unfair, but most of us expect others to carry around a burdensome "unscrambler" for our coded messages.

To say what we mean, and say it straight, must be our constant goal in order for those around us to be able to discard all decoding devices.

Notes

1. Text from PEANUTS by Charles M. Schulz, © 1975 by United Feature Syndicate, Inc. Used by permission.
2. Julius Fritze, *The Essence of Marriage* (Grand Rapids, Mich.: Zondervan Publishing House, 1969), p. 65.
3. H. Norman Wright, *Communication, Key to Your Marriage* (Glendale, Calif.: Regal Books, 1974), p. 53.
4. Wright, p. 54.

CHAPTER TWELVE

CHOOSING TO LISTEN WITH UNDERSTANDING

by Jack and Carole

JACK

We had dinner with a young couple one evening, and their conversation reminded me of a verbal tennis match. The problem was that they were not playing the game with each other. It was more like they were playing with different tennis ball machines.

He started in on a topic of interest to him. She interrupted and took off on another track. A moment later, he interrupted her and went back to his original subject. She then broke in on him, and on and on it went.

The most startling thing about this conversation, if you can call it that, was that this had become such an ingrained pattern they were unaware of what they were doing.

It has been said that listening intently with one's mouth completely and firmly shut is a basic communication skill needed in all marriages. Most of us are so concerned about getting our own ideas across that we only concentrate on the talking aspect of the conversation. We talk *to* people, not *with* them. In doing this, we fail to listen to the other person.

To grow in our love we must develop a special kind of listening—one that hears the words and understands the meaning.

Asking clarifying questions will help the latter. The story is told of a little boy who came to his mother and asked, "Mommy, where did I come from?"

Having heard that when children are old enough to ask that question, they should be told, she thought, "Here goes!" and proceeded to explain the whole complicated process of reproduction. The boy got more and more puzzled throughout her monologue.

When she had finally finished her dissertation, he said, "No, no, Mommy. I mean, where did I come from? Like Jimmy comes from Chicago."

WHY LISTENING IS OF CRITICAL IMPORTANCE

One: It is necessary for a happy marriage.
To be listened to is critical in order to share deeply and sharing deeply is essential for intimacy and happiness.

"Deep sharing is overwhelming, and very rare," writes Paul Tournier. "A thousand fears keep us in check. First of all there is the fear of breaking down, of crying. There is especially the fear that the other will not sense the tremendous importance with which this memory or feeling is charged. How painful it is when such a difficult sharing falls flat, upon ears either preoccupied or mocking, ears in any case that do not sense the significance of what we're saying."[1]

Another experienced counselor was asked, "What is the essential characteristic of a happy marriage?"

"After love," he replied, "the ability to confide fully, freely, and frankly in each other."

Two: Listening helps us become more Christlike as God uses us to sharpen one another.
"No position in life offers more chance for advancement and maturity than marriage," states John Dresher, "yet here we are most afraid to face ourselves." He goes on to say: "Who knows you

better, your weaknesses and strengths, than the person to whom you are married? Who is more interested in making you a better person than the one whose very life depends on you? What better sounding board could you find to test your thoughts, ideas and plans?"[2]

God leads two people together so one can compensate for the other's weaknesses. If we refuse to listen to the person who loves us the most and has our best interests at heart, not only will we fail to be "sharpened" by that relationship, our very prayers could be hindered. Peter cautions husbands in 1 Peter 3:7 (NIV): "Husbands, in the same way be considerate as you live with your wives, and treat them with respect as the weaker partner and as heirs with you of the gracious gift of life, so that nothing will hinder your prayers." In verse 8 he sums up by exhorting "all" to be harmonious, sympathetic, loving, kind-hearted, and humble. How can our lives be harmonious, how can we be truly kind and understanding, if we do not listen to our partner? And if we are not understanding, God says our very communication with Him might be hindered.

We also might end up a nervous wreck! Amos 3:3 says, "Can two walk together, except they be agreed?" (KJV). Living with someone twenty-four hours a day who disagrees with you about important issues will affect your physical, mental, or emotional health.

WHAT HAS HELPED ME TO LISTEN
(CAROLE)

I tend to want to talk more than to listen. It is a habit that is quite ingrained, but God has been faithful to remind me of it. So it is exciting to see how He can root out an irritating habit if we ask Him, as long as we obey Him when He speaks to us.

I have found that memorizing Scripture is one of the best ways to have God speak to my heart. I've also learned the validity of the statement, "I used to memorize Scripture, but now I learn it by heart." In the past, I had sporadically memorized the Word of God for Sunday school contests and classes. But years ago when I started "learning it by heart" consistently and asking God to apply it to my everyday happenings, it changed my life.

It was after I had memorized Proverbs 18:2 that God started poking me quite frequently on the matter of listening to understand. Solomon said, "A fool does not delight in understanding, but only in revealing his own mind." When I would mentally be sitting on the edge of my chair just waiting for someone to finish so I could put my two cents worth in, God would remind me, "Carole, a fool does not delight in understanding, but only in revealing her own mind."

I'd say, "Ouch," and then ask God to help me really listen to understand.

Some wives feel their husbands rarely listen to them. Often, it's nothing they've done, but a periodic "check-up" may be helpful to ask *why*. We may need to ask God to search our hearts and try our thoughts to discover if there are bad habits, unkind words, and critical attitudes which are causing husbands—and perhaps others—not to listen to us (see Psalm 139:23-24).

A woman once told me, "My husband never listens to me. I could talk all day and he wouldn't hear a word I said!"

Well, I listened. It was a difficult task, but I did listen. For over an hour I listened to a woman who was hypercritical, sarcastic, and negative . . . and I felt sorry for that husband. She had built a climate of criticism into her marriage, and he had simply tuned her out. I had to admit that if I had been in his shoes, I'd have probably done the same thing.

Most of us interrupt a conversation now and then and it's no big deal. But if interrupting has become a way of life with us, it can be infuriating to a mate as well as to others. Dedicating ourselves to stopping this practice could go a long way in the battle to listen intently. Can this insidious habit be broken? Yes, if we ask help from God and from our mates. In private conversation (never,

never in public, please), when our spouse interrupts, point it out. In love. Keep pointing it out to each other till the habit is broken. Pray together concerning an attitude of oneness to allow for correction from the other partner. Ask for *God's power* to break the habit, for it must be broken.

God will help us be the kind of person worth listening to. The Bible says that the mouth of the righteous is a "well of life" (Proverbs 10:11, KJV). (I admit to sometimes wondering if mine is more like a babbling brook!) Our creative God can and will give us truth worth sharing as we surrender to the Holy Spirit who gives us His fruit of love . . . and joy . . . and peace . . . and makes our mouths wells of life.

To listen and to be listened to is essential to communication. Only as we develop these traits will we really begin to understand each other and gain inroads into the mind and heart of the person whom God chose for us and of whom He said, "These two . . . shall become *one*."

Notes

1. Paul Tournier, *To Understand Each Other* (Atlanta, Ga.: John Knox Press, 1967), pp. 28-29.
2. John Drescher, "Formula for a Happy Marriage," *Christian Life* (July 1970), p. 28.

CHAPTER THIRTEEN

CHOOSING TO BE OPEN

by Carole

We were just finishing the breakfast dishes when Jack walked into the kitchen. "Where are my keys?" he asked hurriedly.

"In the top drawer," I responded.

"Those are *your* keys," he argued.

"No, they are yours," I countered emphatically. I had just had a new set made, so I was *positive* about whose keys were in that drawer. Convinced, he took them, thanked me, and walked out.

The young wife helping me with the dishes that morning had been visiting us for a few days. She turned to me with a thoughtful expression on her face and said, "Carole, I wish you would pray for me."

"I'd be happy to pray for you," I replied. "But how do you want me to pray?"

She answered sadly, "When my husband asks me a question the way Jack just asked you, he sounds angry."

"Oh?" I murmured. "Well, does he just sound angry or is he angry?"

After a moment's hesitation, she said sorrowfully, "I don't know."

"I don't know." These words echoed a hollow refrain in my mind. I shook my head in wonder. We knew this couple well. Her concerns about her husband's state of mind were not new. Yet when he would ask her about something and sound angry, her questions were left unasked. Constantly his tone of voice had shouted to her that he was angry with her.

To have intimacy in a marriage we *must* learn to communicate all the time, even when we are hurt . . . or frustrated . . . or angry.

This wife had never asked her husband the simple question, "Are you angry?" Instead she had assumed his anger, and her assumption was that he was angry with *her*. She felt insecure and unhappy—two feelings that had been growing within her for years.

All she needed was to ask her husband, "Are you angry?" This question would have communicated that he sounded angry to her and, if he wasn't, perhaps he needed to do something about the tone of his voice. If he really was angry and answered yes to her question, she undoubtedly would then have needed to ask, "Are you angry at me?" (It could have been that he had accidentally stubbed his toe in the bathroom and was mad at himself.)

This couple needed to get their feelings out of all the musty closets of their lives and spring clean their marital house. Most of our difficulties come from misunderstanding one another because we won't talk and bring all those moldy things out into the open air. Instead, we seem to be content to read into one another's words, tone of voice, or silence, and we usually are very poor readers. A simple, clarifying question would save us hours, weeks, and even years of heartache and misunderstanding. Conflicts come because we haven't found out what the other person means. Counselors generally agree that there are five levels in communication. John Powell, well-known writer on interpersonal relationships, words them as follows:

Level 5—Cliché conversation
Level 4—Reporting the facts about others

Level 3 — My ideas and judgments
Level 2 — My feelings (emotions)
Level 1 — Peak communication[1]

Real communication begins at level three — my ideas and judgments. It is at this point that a person is willing to step out of his self-imposed solitary confinement and take a risk by telling a personal idea or thought to another person. He may still be cautious and, if he senses that what he is saying is not being accepted or listened to, he will retreat. If I tell you about an idea I have and you say, "That's dumb," it will be the last time I will share an idea with you. I have taken a risk and have been rejected. I may not risk again.

Level three then leads into and develops into levels two and one. Peak communication is when there is consistent and total empathy and understanding between two people.

In an everyday situation, the depth of levels in communication may work something like this:

The husband walks in the front door after work and his wife says, "Hi! How was your day?" This is level five — cliché conversation.

The husband answers, "Oh, okay." For some couples their big conversation of the day has just occurred.

But this wife wants to dialogue, so she asks, "How did the meeting go this afternoon?"

Her husband responds, "Fair." Now we are at level four — reporting the facts. However, the question was a poor one. We have a "family joke" in our household about questions that can be answered with one word, because if they can be, they will be. A better question would have been, "What was the most important thing you discussed at your meeting?" or, "What was the attitude of the president toward your plan?"

The wife may now try to get to the feeling level (level two) by asking, "How did you feel the meeting went this afternoon?" only to have the husband respond on the third level with an idea or judgment. He may respond, "In my opinion, the committee came up with the wrong answers."

So she tries again, "Was that frustrating to you?"

"Yes," the husband declares. "I really felt badly that they hadn't done a better job of thinking through."

Now the couple is at a feeling level—the point of real communication . . . of talking of needs, disappointments, hopes, dreams. They may break through at any moment to level one—the open, total sharing with all defenses down.

That level might be reached when the man says, "I'm feeling so discouraged right now at my inability to help those men think through on the subject thoroughly. They aren't a team at all and somehow that has to be my fault. I seem to be inadequate for the job." And his wife accepts that empathetically, does not criticize his feeling that way, and begins working with him to overcome what he thinks are his inadequacies.

David Augsburger has said:

> Communication is the meeting of meaning. When your meaning meets my meaning across the bridge of words, tones, acts, and deeds, when understanding occurs, then we know that we have communicated. . . .
>
> When two persons can share from the very center of their existence, they experience love in its truest quality. Marriage is a venture into intimacy, and intimacy is the opening of one self to another.[2]

The Apostle Paul sums up our goal which is not to be immature children, but to speak the truth in love and to grow up into Christ (Ephesians 4:15). If all our conversations could be judged by that one phrase—"speaking the truth in love"—we would have both total and complete honesty and the kind of sensitive love we need to hear the real questions our wives or husbands are asking.

Being "totally transparent" and "speaking the truth in love" are quite different. Some people advocate the kind of transparency where we say everything that pops into our heads. Some feel we can't even know our own feelings unless we share them aloud with others. I disagree. Thoughts that are unkind and unloving, and attitudes that would burden the person to whom they might be ventilated, are best shared with God alone.

This is not to infer that we cannot share negatives. We can and we must. But negatives must also be shared in love. It is not loving to share things that cannot be changed. It might be true that I don't especially care for your big nose, but it is not kind or loving to tell you so. We must accept and overlook things that cannot be changed. Solomon put it this way: "My son, never forget the things I've taught you. . . . Never forget to be truthful and kind. Hold these virtues tightly. Write them deep within your heart" (Proverbs 3:1-3, TLB).

Both "speaking the truth" and "in love" have to be considered. Those two statements need to be married forever and ever in our speech.

Perhaps, the greatest deterrent for most to speak honestly and kindly is *ridicule*. It would be for me.

You see, on some small back burner of my mind, an idea is always simmering. Most of these, when strained through Jack's objective colander, are without substance, but now and then I come up with a solid thought. If Jack ever ridiculed the worthless ideas, I'd have stopped verbalizing any of them long ago. But because of his understanding and acceptance, the creative concoctions of my mind simmer away happily.

His refusal to belittle even my wildest ideas has been a great help on our journey to intimacy. His acceptance of my thinking processes causes me to love him more deeply and helps me to be me. To be accepted unconditionally by another person is a freeing thing. One of the wonderful things about being a Christian is to know that God Himself accepts me totally and unconditionally when I come to Him through Christ. Jack has been an example to me of Christ's love in this way through the years.

When people are ridiculed, they often pull their heads into their shells and don't venture to stick them out again. But to know and be known are essential to love and intimacy. So even though I may be afraid, I must take the risk . . . again and again and again . . . of exposing my tender skin to a possible verbal blade and, putting my trust in God, hazard another possible hurt or rejection.

Not only is the road to intimacy blocked by ridicule, it is also obstructed by the wall of protective silence that I build around my feelings. The problem with building walls to keep hurt out is that the wall isolates me also.

Sometimes building that wall is a totally unconscious thing. "Nothing is wrong" is a phrase that Jack and I have been trying to rid from our vocabulary. It is hard to do—especially for me.

When Jack does something that hurts or offends me, the first tactic to which I resort is silence. Being a rather loquacious person, Jack immediately senses something is wrong when I am quiet. Which is why I am quiet! If he didn't ask me about it, I would get worse. Knowing this, he is forced to ask, "Is there anything wrong?"

My answer is, "No."

"Are you sure?" he persists

"Yes," I lie.

"Come on, honey. I can tell something is bothering you. What is it?"

"Nothing," I respond. And on and on and on we go.

Basically, I guess, I don't tell him on the first go-round because I am either a bit ashamed at the silliness of the whole thing or I don't think Jack has suffered enough yet.

Childish? Yes.

Immature? Certainly.

Fair? Definitely not.

Whatever it is, I need to get it out. To say, "Yes, there is something wrong, but it is so inconsequential and silly that I am ashamed to tell you. I'd like the opportunity to get over it first."

Or, "Yes, but if I tell you right now, I'll cry, so please wait a few minutes."

Or even, "I'm not sure what's wrong. I think I really do feel like being quiet for a change. It has nothing to do with you."

A word of explanation is needed for love's sake. It will get your partner off the hook, or bring the problem out in the open. Either way, the loving, mature thing to do is to tear down the wall of silent hostility and expose it to God's cleansing light.

In our marriage, I am most guilty of using the "silent treatment." But it is often the husband who retreats into silence. One of the most sorrowful cries I hear from wives is, "My husband won't talk to me."

Cecil Osborne, counselor and former pastor, said,

> A woman's need for a close relationship is so great that if she cannot achieve it one way, she will instinctively try another. If her efforts at communication are balked by the husband's silence, she has all sorts of alternatives at her disposal: she may become angry over a trifle, or accusatory, or depressed. In an almost frantic attempt to force some kind of communication she will push any button on his control panel; if he finally erupts with anger, she will feel that she at least has gotten some response. . . . At a totally unconscious level the wife is saying, "I'd like first class love. If I cannot have that, I'll settle for attention. If I fail to get your attention, I'll get your sympathy. If that fails, I'll get you where it hurts—I'll have an accident or a symptom.[3]

I often wonder if men realize that when some wives pick a fight deliberately, it could be their way of saying they need attention, some response. But all too often silence is used by men and women as a tool to frustrate and punish.

With the help of God, we can grow to be mature enough not

to use silence as a weapon, to rid ourselves of ridicule, and to understand that marriage, as an adventure into intimacy, takes a great deal of work. We'll never attain perfect openness this side of Heaven, but strive for it we must.

John Powell realistically states the task:

> My person is not a little hard core inside of me, a little fully-formed statue that is real and authentic, permanent and fixed; my person rather implies a dynamic process. In other words, if you knew me yesterday, please do not think that it is the same person that you are meeting today.
>
> I have experienced more of life. I have encountered new depths in those I love, I have suffered and prayed, and I am different. . . . Approach me, then, with a sense of wonder, study my face and hands and voice for signs of change; for it is certain that I have changed.[4]

Notes
1. John Powell, *Why Am I Afraid to Tell You Who I Am?* (Niles, Ill.: Argus Communications, 1969), pp. 50-62.
2. David W. Augsburger, *Cherishable: Love and Marriage* (Scottsdale, Penn.: Herald Press, 1971), pp. 54-55.
3. From *The Art of Understanding Your Mate* by Cecil Osborne, p. 53. Copyright 1970 Zondervan Publishing House, Grand Rapids, Mich. Used by permission.
4. Powell, pp. 50-62.

CHAPTER FOURTEEN

CHOOSING CONSTRUCTIVE CONFLICT

by Carole

U-R-P. You've never heard of it, right? (Or did you think I'd just hiccuped?) Vernon Cronen, a professor of communication studies at the University of Massachusetts, coined the term in 1979.[1] The initials stand for Unwanted Repetitive Patterns, which is a fancy way of saying that we tend to get stuck in a rut in the way we fight, mostly because of the way we've been wired together from day one.

There are as many ways to fight as there are personalities. Some simmer; some explode. Some attack head-on, others blindside. But two opposing styles we are all familiar with are what some call the confronter and the avoider, or the attacker and the retreater. Others label these dual approaches the expressive and the nonexpressive: "Usually the nonexpressive person will want to walk away from conflict, while the expressive wants to talk about it, find out what's wrong, and be friends again . . . nonexpressives do not want to talk about it, and believe that if they don't, it will go away. They feel if they just let it alone, everyone will remain friends."[2]

Whatever you name them, they're easy to identify, and so are their techniques.

The positive aspect of what we'll call the confronter is that conflict issues are brought out into the open, talked about, and ideally, worked through to a conclusion. But confronters want to confront *right now*—anytime, anywhere, and anything—and sometimes their timing is *awful*.

The withdrawer knows that at times silence is golden because issues can look monstrous when you're tired, sick, or struggling with other pressing problems. Sometimes a little distance is all you need to see that the Creature from the Lost Lagoon is really just a small, ordinary toad.

Both types, however, often use unfair techniques.

The confronter is frequently an expert at bringing up the past and adept at hauling in secondary issues.

The expressives tend to exaggerate and intimidate. They may yell, scream, and even use an "ultimate" threat such as, "Well, maybe we ought to get a divorce," or "You'd like me to commit suicide, wouldn't you?"

Some may also use humiliation to intimidate with exaggerated statements such as "How can you be so stupid?"

Withdrawers have their own *modus operandi*. Obviously, the overall approach is to duck the confrontation in any way possible—being too busy to talk, postponing the discussion, mumbling "Why don't we talk about this another time?" or "Let's not make a big deal out of this."

When forced, they will often sidestep the issue by (1) changing the subject, (2) interrupting and thus not allowing the other to finish the statement, (3) crying, or (4) waving the white flag of surrender before the discussion is over. Withdrawers may also simply refuse to talk about it, ignore it, sulk, pout, or give the cold shoulder for days on end.

Both confronters and withdrawers use the tactic of sarcasm and ridicule. Both may be quick to jump to a conclusion, try to read the other's mind, grab the old standbys "always" and "never," or use cold logic in refusing to deal with hot emotions.

If both partners are withdrawers, a marriage's growth and intimacy are in great danger. If both are confronters, heads may roll! The ideal seems to be to have one confronter and one withdrawer with *both* being willing to learn from the personality of the other. The confronter needs to learn timing, peacemaking, and tact. The withdrawer needs to learn honesty, the ability to share feelings, and discipline to face issues as they come up.

Why? In order to obey God. God tells us to speak the truth in love (Ephesians 4:15), which is both an admonition to unloving confronters to speak in *love*, and also a command to withdrawers to *speak*.

Scripture abounds in instructions concerning conflict, such as "faithful are the wounds of a friend" (Proverbs 27:6); "admonish one another with all wisdom" (Colossians 3:16, NIV); "keep short accounts" (my paraphrase of Ecclesiastes 8:11, NIV, "When the sentence for a crime is not quickly carried out, the hearts of the people are filled with schemes to do wrong"); and "If your brother sins, go and reprove him in private" (Matthew 18:15). These commands for *all* Christians are especially necessary between spouses.

SOME "REMEMBERS" BEFORE YOU START

Whether we are withdrawers or confronters, God has established some rules for our behavior in the midst of conflict. Let me suggest a study in the book of Proverbs to find your own list, but here are a few principles from *The Living Bible* to start you off. Review these "remembers" from Proverbs to prepare yourself when you know you're heading into a conflict situation:

Remember to keep cool. It's been said that emotions have to be cooled until the fight takes the form of a problem to be solved. As Proverbs puts it: "A fool is quick-tempered; a wise man stays cool when insulted" (12:16).

Remember to lower your voice instead of raising it. "A soft answer turns away wrath, but harsh words cause quarrels" (15:1).

Remember to think before you speak. "Self-control means controlling the tongue! A quick retort can ruin everything" (13:3).

Remember to be kind and humble. "Pride leads to arguments; be humble, take advice and become wise" (13:10).

Both withdrawers and confronters need godly maturity to avoid trying to "win" a battle. Confronters want to win by overpowering the other person; yet God would not have us be guilty of either power-grabbing or character assassination. Withdrawers want to win by silence. Not only must we be careful of our motive in a conflict, but we must avoid arguments that are not allowed to *end*.

JUST WHAT IS THE PROBLEM, ANYWAY?

Now we move from *approaching* the conflict to *identifying* the conflict. Have you, as a couple, ever put down on paper what your conflicts are actually about — by subject matter? For instance, are the majority of your fights about irritating habits, discipline of children, money, in-laws, sex, unmet needs, religion, vacations, use of time, and so on?

Jack and I are convinced that a great percentage of conflicts are not *real* conflicts at all, but a matter of misunderstanding. A husband asks if his wife has a new dress on, thinking it looks great, but she interprets the question as saying she's spent too much money. And away we go.

Another large percentage of conflicts come under the "hidden agenda" kind of fight that requires patience and multiple attempts to find the way beneath the surface to the *real* issue — an issue of which even the person beginning it may be unaware. A wife picks a fight because her husband forgot to take out the garbage, but the real issue is her desire for more physical affection. In fact, the desire for more love and affection is probably the number one problem beneath the surface of many quarrels. Years ago, one older wife observed profoundly, "I wish men would realize that many times when wives are unhappy, irritable, or ready to pick a fight, they really need a reassurance of their husband's love." After years of observation, I'd say she was right on.

I still have difficulty at times telling Jack in a direct way what I'm feeling or needing. Because, after all, to *tell* him that I need a hug would somehow take away from its effectiveness. To *tell* him that I need more time talking in depth would reveal that my need is greater than his, and that—horrible thought!—I need him more than he needs me. And so I withdraw and puff on my need with little hurting breaths until Jack becomes aware of my gloom and asks me what is the matter. Or some *unrelated* argument starts and the whole smelly pot boils over.

Then even when he asks me, I will likely give a vague and irrelevant answer—also unfair. Instead of stating my needs directly—"Honey, I'm really feeling like the whole world is trying to shoot me down and I need you to hold me for a few minutes"—I just hint at them—"Oh, it's been a terrible day, but I'll be okay." I want Jack to *know* what I need without my telling him because to tell him is a bit humiliating or embarrassing. Many wives excel in this little game of "He should know what I mean or need."

I've also been guilty of stating a request in a negative rather than the positive form. I might say, "I haven't left the house all day," rather than "Would you mind watching the children for thirty minutes so I can take a walk?" Or "I don't have anything in the house for dinner," instead of saying, "Honey, do you suppose we could go out for a bite to eat tonight?"

Identifying the *real* problem when conflict arises is a crucial step toward resolution. Here is a series of steps that we've found helpful:

Define the problem or issue of disagreement. Sometimes this step can get complicated. Often a couple doesn't get to the real issue on the first go-round. A prior step could be taking it individually to the Lord and praying for His wisdom to define the dispute specifically. James 1:5 (NIV) states, "If any of you lacks wisdom, he should ask God, who gives generously to all without finding fault, and it will be given to him."

Some will find it helpful to write their thoughts out on paper after they've prayed, and go through several sessions of thinking and praying before they are able to define the true difficulty.

Agreeing on the precise nature of the disagreement may take several sessions as well. But stick with it until you both agree on the exact issue.

How does each of you contribute to the problem? Be as honest as you can about your Unwanted Repetitive Patterns here. Own up to any unfair techniques.

Brainstorm and list all possible solutions. Be creative on this, and don't ridicule even the craziest ideas. What could each of you do differently the next time to avoid repeating this same problem?

Discuss each solution and agree on one to try. Make sure you're both clear on what the change will be and how expectations need to be adjusted accordingly. Agree on how each person will work toward the solution.

Set a time to review your progress. If you haven't hit upon the perfect solution the first time, try another of your solutions or go back to step three and try again. But of course, the whole thing breaks down if you aren't willing to come to grips with the basic issue that is causing the conflict in the first place.

Many marriage counselors believe that, except in rare instances, the specific complaint named by squabbling partners is merely a symptom of a deeper conflict between them. Obviously, unless a couple understands what they are fighting about and are willing to deal with the underlying cause, their arguments will continue.

But sometimes the underlying cause is so deeply buried, it's not evident—at least on the conscious level. Some heart-searching questions may need to be asked . . . before God. Begin by praying Psalm 139:23-24, "Search me, O God, and know my heart; try me and know my anxious thoughts; and see if there is any hurtful way in me, and lead me in the everlasting way." Isn't that terrific? God really can help us know ourselves. He can reveal *me* to me!

One of the first questions I need to ask Him is about that "underlying cause." Exactly *why* am I so furious? What is the true issue here?

A primary factor may involve *control* issues. Ask yourself, "Am I irritable and quarrelsome because I need to feel in *control* of our relationship in some way?" This is a factor more often than we might like to admit. Sometimes when a wife goes back to work, for instance, a husband subconsciously feels threatened and starts to pick at things he never did before simply because he feels he's lost control.

A second question to ask of the Lord in discerning root issues concerns *attitude*—about life, my partner, my marriage. Am I focusing attention on the problems in our relationship and neglecting the positive factors that brought us together?

A third diagnostic question could be, "Is this a time of crisis that is putting extra pressure on our relationship?" Some areas of conflict are to be expected at certain stages in the marital lifecycle—such as a new baby, a move, a death in the family, loss of a job, or health problems.

There may be times when we need the guidance of a marriage counselor, a pastor, or an older Christian to help us uncover the root cause of repeated quarrels. Proverbs urges us to use godly counsel. A mature couple will go for needed help quickly. Books can be helpful if we make the effort to read them, preferably aloud together, sorting through what the real issues are.

HOW DO WE HANDLE IT?

Now let's move from *identifying* conflict to *handling* conflict. Here are some overall guidelines:

Focus on the beautiful. Whole books have been written about thinking positively, but the Bible says it best: "Finally, brethren, whatever is true, whatever is honorable, whatever is right, whatever is pure, whatever is lovely, whatever is of good repute, if there is any excellence and if anything worthy of praise, let your mind dwell on these things" (Philippians 4:8). But what do you and I give our attention to? Usually, what we'd like to see changed, what we don't like, and those things that don't please us.

Scripture makes it clear that we become what we think about. Think negatively, and you become a negative person.

Try listing all the wonderful qualities you appreciate in your spouse—whatever made you fall in love in the first place. Read the list every day and add to it. Pick one quality to share with your partner daily with a special compliment. Use your list for a "Thank You, God" prayer time. Talk with your spouse about the pleasures you've shared during your marriage, the mutual goals you wish to reach.

Refuse to "win" an argument. "Winning" is really losing because you haven't broken through to better understanding of each other and the situation.

Learn to communicate ideas and feelings more clearly. Work at the art of dialogue until you can explain to the other's satisfaction what *the other one* is feeling and saying. Or you might try "role reversal"—switch sides in arguments, or do each other's chores for a while so you can understand what your partner contends with on a daily basis.

Be very careful about venting hostile feelings. "Letting it all hang out" usually just increases both persons' anger and aggravates the problem that triggered it. It seldom helps a couple come to grips intelligently with the basic reason for their fight.

Study your partner's differences. Learn from these, respect them.

Never underestimate the power of praying together. God really is in the business of answering prayer. He can break through our stubborn spirits if we give Him the opportunity. I know it's hard to invite Him in when a quarrel is in process, but if we will do it, He will surprise us with joy and forgiveness.

And remember, you can't change anyone. Only God can. Openness to God's changes in our *own* lives is vital.

Make physical contact. One counselor suggests you face each other when you quarrel with knees touching, holding hands. Hard to shout, exaggerate, and accuse in that position, isn't it?

Forgive. Ah, that's a tough one, isn't it? But God's unconditional forgiveness to us is the basis of His command to forgive others unconditionally. We are to forgive over and over again; before we pray; when the other repents; for the sake of Christ and to defeat Satan; as Christ forgave us; and with a heart of love.[3]

Go beyond forgiveness to understanding. Stay with the argument—or come back to it as much as needed when the emotions have subsided somewhat—until you both understand from the the other's point of view *why* it happened. Perhaps it was just a bad mood that happens occasionally to all of us, but knowing and understanding the effect of a mood on your spouse is also valuable. Keep exploring until the *good* aspects of those differences have been discovered.

Don't waste a good fight! You can grow by determining to use conflict to know your spouse.

LEARN TO BE RESOLVERS

In review of this in-depth look at confronters and withdrawers in conflict, let's emphasize the goal of *resolving*. To that end, we present "The Five Rs":

1. *Repeat* to each other what the quarrel is really about. Write it out if necessary, redefining it until both of you agree. This in itself will resolve a good many arguments.
2. *Release* it to God in prayer—separately and together. It is difficult to stay angry when you are taking it to the Lord.

3. *Reason* it through together. Use the steps we listed in this chapter as a guide for identifying the problem as well as possible solutions.
4. *Resolve* and *leave* it. When it's over, move beyond it. Admit your mistakes, learn from criticism, and start fresh.
5. *Rebuild* the relationship afterwards. "Love forgets mistakes; nagging about them parts the best of friends" (Proverbs 17:9, TLB).

If your partner is unwilling to work toward a solution, some of these steps will still help—defining the difficulty, praying about it, forgiving even when the other hasn't asked forgiveness. Ask God for His wisdom on timing—when or if to bring it up again, what the next step is, what you alone can do to improve the situation and continue building the relationship in other areas. Above all, ask for wisdom in knowing when to speak and when to be still, for discerning if the issue should be forced into the open or put behind you unresolved.

If both of you are willing to work at conflict resolution, then you are ready to learn how to turn every argument into a *discussion*. And boy, is that hard!

To fight—that's okay.

To fight fairly—that's growth.

But to fight with kindness and love—that's grace!

Notes
1. Norma Peterson, "How to Stop Fighting and Start Loving Again," *McCall's* (August 1983), p. 8.
2. Chuck and Barb Snyder, *Incompatibility: Grounds for a Great Marriage* (Sisters, Oreg.: Questar Publishers, 1988), p. 115.
3. Matthew 18:21, Mark 11:25-26, Luke 17:3-4, 2 Corinthians 2:10, Ephesians 4:32, Colossians 3:13.

CHAPTER FIFTEEN

CHOOSING TO ACT LOVINGLY

by Jack and Carole

JACK

One day a few years into our marriage, Carole let me know that we needed to have a Big Discussion. You know the kind. No little spur-of-the-moment verbal exchange, but a Serious Talk. I tend to want to delay these as long as possible, but I'd learned by then that this was not wise.

The conversation went something like this:

"You know, sweetheart," Carole began, "I'm beginning to wonder about something. It seems to me that usually I'm the one to initiate touching, hugging, kissing—that kind of affection. And I've had the growing feeling that this is not something you enjoy. Sometimes you appear almost embarrassed by it. Other times, you seem to brush it away and merely stand there."

She paused, trying to choose her words carefully. "I know that touching and affection are not necessarily barometers of love, and I know you love me. But I don't want to be doing something that you don't like or that embarrasses you. I have to admit, touching is important to me, but I want to please you and I will try to change in this area if you want me to."

CAROLE

He makes it sound much more controlled than I remember it! I cried buckets of tears over this, and prayed, and cried some more. Then I pleaded for God's wisdom and, punctuated with pauses to wipe my eyes, the Serious Talk began.

JACK

I swallowed. What she said was true. At times when I came home, she would greet me with an exuberant hug and kiss and I'd just stand there like a telephone pole. Apparently, Carole had gotten tired of hugging a telephone pole.

I was brought up in a home in which love was not expressed with a lot of hugging and kissing although I knew my parents loved me. Carole's home was just the opposite. The usual way of saying "thanks" or "you're great" or "I love you" was a big bear hug and a kiss. Often touchers and non-touchers end up married to one another.

However, my reserve wasn't simply a product of my family background. I tend to be more restrained in expressing any emotion, not just affection. It isn't that I don't have strong emotions, I just don't wear them in public.

It didn't take me long to realize what my response should be on this one, however. You see, I liked the affectionate nature of my wife. I enjoyed her touches, hugs, and kisses. So I said, "Honey, I'm sorry you have felt that I don't like your affection. I'll have to admit, because of my background and nature, I am a bit embarrassed at times—when you kiss me in public or in front of company. But I like it! So please don't change. Don't stop."

I knew that I needed to go still one more step, and so I added, "In fact, I want to learn to be more affectionate toward you—to be at ease in expressing emotion even in public. So be patient with me and help me learn."

And she was and did. She became my hugging and kissing coach (and I was an apt pupil). Now, after all these years, I can hug and kiss with the best of them!

The more we read and study and have experienced life, the more I am grateful that God helped me to be willing to change. I no longer feel awkward in some of the social situations in which we find ourselves. I don't feel ill at ease when the culture of a country demands a hug and a kiss on both cheeks—when you come and when you go—or with hostesses who expect a hug upon arrival. Touching has become a part of me and a part of growing.

Carole and I see increasing evidence of the great need that most humans have just to be touched. In *Love Life for Every Married Couple*, Dr. Ed Wheat states,

> God created us with hundreds of thousands of microscopic nerve endings in our skin designed to sense and benefit from a loving touch. A tender touch tells us that we are cared for. It can calm our fears, soothe pain, bring us comfort, or give us the blessed satisfaction of emotional security. As adults, touching continues to be a primary means of communicating with those we love, whether we are conscious of it or not. Our need for a caring touch is normal and healthy and we will never outgrow it. . . . Physical contact is absolutely essential in building the emotion of love. You may take it as a sobering warning that most of the time marital infidelity is not so much a search for sex as it is for emotional intimacy.[1]

Just recently Carole and I talked to a couple where the man said, "I need more affection. She doesn't touch me or seem to have a need to be touched. I long for more physical touching, hugs, and kisses."

There was more going on in this marriage than lack of affection on the wife's part, and we discovered some reasons why she was pulling away from her husband, but here was a wife who needed to work on being outwardly demonstrative and affectionate.

Mostly, however, it seems women have the greater desire for more nonsexual touching, for tenderness, for romance.

In a cartoon by Lynn Johnson, a wife asks her husband (who, his back toward her, is resting on the couch), "Do you take me for granted, John? Have we been married so long that the passion has gone out of our relationship?" By this time he is sitting up sleepily on the couch, and she's shaking him. "Do you look at me with the same sense of longing that you had when we first fell in love?"

The last frame shows him staggering away saying, "Wait. I'll get my glasses."[2]

A reader wrote to a national magazine with the question, "Is romance dead after marriage?" She went on to say that, in her experience and most of her friends' experience, there is no romance left after several years of marriage. She missed those warm feelings. "There is a very special part of women that periodically requires the nourishment of romance," she wrote.

The writer of the article wisely called this reader and several of her friends and their husbands for a conference. While the women were in one room complaining about the lack of romance in their lives, the men were in another saying things like:

"It's something I want as much as she does. Listen—before we were married I used to get all kinds of indications from her that I was recognized as somebody special, that I was wanted. The fact that we're married now doesn't mean that I'm willing to take that for granted. I still want those signals from her that say she wants me and finds me exciting."

One ponytailed mother of two young children, sitting cross-legged on the floor, tried to tell why she felt so good about her marriage. "He confirms me as a woman," she explained, "and I think I confirm him as a man."

The author said, "Is that what romance is all about? Is that why it's so important to feel actively desired and consciously pursued? Seen in those terms, romance is far more than the lost giddiness of courtship. It is that completed sense of our womanliness, that fulfillment of our sexuality in and out of the bedroom. It is feeling good about ourselves, feeling confirmed as women."[3]

This article indicates that both men and women want romance, some more actively than others and certainly in different ways. Women want the unexpected, the intensity of desire, the romantic setting—a walk on a moonlit beach, a candlelight dinner in a quaint chalet, a blanket spread under a grove of trees. But even those things wouldn't be romantic if the talk is business, problems, the kids. No, the conversation has to be about the two of them, about love, about wonderful memories, about desire.

Generally, men's ideas of "romance" and women's ideas are poles apart. When Carole asked me what came to my mind as romantic, I named several places, like having hot chocolate in our room overlooking Hong Kong Harbor. Her first thoughts were of moods.

Dr. Ed Wheat describes five kinds of love and how each can be worked on.[4] One kind of love is "eros," which is romantic love. The other kinds are sexual love, friendship love, security love, and giving or agape love. When there is betrayal or unfaithfulness, trust is destroyed and the security kind of love vanishes. This will, of course, affect romantic love. When struggles come in sexual love, romantic love is also affected. However, even when sexual love and secure love are strong, romantic love can be in a pitiful state.

Each kind of love must be worked on. There is no letting up! If a woman says that she loves gardening, but she never does any planting, watering, and weeding, then her talk about love is meaningless.

Many wives and husbands need to begin to water their garden—to work at romance, affection, and intimacy.

For Carole, a great part of keeping the romance in our marriage comes from touching. Cuddling. Eye contact when we hear something funny. An unexpected hug. After one man hugged his wife, the dots on her dress burst into bloom! (Actually, it happened in a cartoon.)

Yes, husbands, touch is that important!

But another way to develop the climate of intimacy in our relationships is by frequent glances at our spouses. This is one way to tell if an engaged couple is really in love with each another. Every joke, profound remark, or inane statement is a cause to glance at the other and share a look. Sadly, most couples begin to lose this eye contact after they have been married a few months. If you have grown less frequent in the deep, long, intimate looks or the quick, let's-share-this look, talk about it and begin to glance at each other often when in group discussion (or even watching television). If the other doesn't glance back, give a nudge (if you're close enough) and soon you may again enjoy the warm feeling of sharing these intimate moments.

"Reserved people need to work on being more demonstrative not just for the sake of others, but for their own sake, for their own balance, maturity, and development," says family counselor Dr. Gary Oliver. "Just as God demonstrated His love for us, part of the process of sanctification involves us learning effective ways to demonstrate our love for one another."[5]

How do reserved people learn to be more expressive and affectionate? Well, logical people take logical steps, right? They get rid of single chairs in front of the television (except for guests, of course). They wouldn't hear of having twin beds or bucket seats in their automobiles. They practice saying hello, good-morning, or good-night with at least a hug if not a kiss.

I read of one mother who got into the habit of asking her children each day if their "loving cup" was full. If they said no, she'd hold them in her arms for a time until they were "filled up." Not a bad idea for married people, either.

I realize that I've written much more about the need for the undemonstrative person to work to meet the needs of the affectionate member, but in this case the responsibility does lie with the reserved one for two reasons: (1) the demonstrative nature can't be stifled without serious negative consequences, and (2) intimacy in a marriage grows deeper with demonstrations of affection and love.

Now some of you reserved people are shaking your heads and saying, "How do I do that? And what about my partner accepting the fact that I am undemonstrative by nature?"

Leighton Ford is quoted as saying, "God loves and accepts us just the way we are, but He loves us too much to leave us that way!"

So once again, change is demanded. And we can describe the key ingredients as communication, compromise, and reform.

Communication

Communication about what is wanted is the first step. Not in generalities, but in specifics. For Carole that takes a lot of thought, because she just has a feeling of what she wants without much thought about what will give her that feeling. Being factual, I need her to tell me specifics.

Take some time to explore with each other questions such as: How important to you is the celebration of special occasions such as birthdays, anniversaries, Valentine's Day? What is your idea of "celebration"? What to you is "romantic"? What would you like for me to do specifically to show affection and care? (Really get down to particulars here, such as: I want you to greet me with a kiss when I come home; I'd like you to hold my hand in public; I'd like you to sit on the couch with me when we watch television.) In these specified items, which is most important to you? Least important?

As you talk to each other about these issues, talk also with God about them. Remember, God is a creative God and will give you new, creative thoughts if you ask Him. He is full of ideas! And He is just waiting to reveal them to you.

Then, too, talk to older people who evidence love in their

marriages. Ask them how they show their partner special love, and write down their answers. Read books.

Compromise

A naturally reserved person is never going to be able to meet all the physical needs that a demonstrative person has to be touched and held, so compromise is necessary. Children and friends help fill the "loving cup" of the affectionate-natured. And so do intimate times spent with God — a God who loves without reserve. True, He doesn't have "skin on," but to feel His arms of love wrapped around us in our spirits is often to have our loving cup filled to overflowing.

Change

We'll keep saying it! The name of the game is change. Perhaps only millimeters at a time — but we can and should be changing. If the affectionate person is changing by learning to have some of those needs met by God and by others; if the reserved person is adding one way of demonstrating affection every few months, then both are growing in understanding and expanding in intimacy.

But whatever steps need taking must be taken!

I hope I hear the logical person saying, "That's true."

I know the intuitive one is declaring, "You bet!"

Is the reserved one saying, "I'll try"?

Maybe not. But I'm sure of one thing. The toucher will say, "Hurray! Let's go for it!"

Notes
1. Ed Wheat, *Love Life for Every Married Couple* (Grand Rapids, Mich.: Zondervan Publishing House, 1980), p. 183.
2. Lynn Johnston, "For Better or For Worse," *Partnership* (January-February 1988), p. 54.
3. Claire Safran, "Must Marriage Kill Romance?" *Redbook* (February 1974), pp. 81-84.
4. Wheat, p. 57.
5. From seminar notes by Dr. Gary Oliver. Used by permission.

CHAPTER SIXTEEN

CHOOSING TO KNOW OUR SPOUSE'S LOVE LANGUAGE

by Carole

Wha hen I opened the door, there stood a small boy, hair growing every which way, looking at me with big brown eyes. He spoke, but whatever he said went right by me. I smiled and stepped back, motioning him to come inside, and called upstairs to my grandson, "Eric! There's someone at the door for you." Then I thought, *I sure hope he's here for Eric, and not selling something.*

For you see, I didn't understand a word the little fellow had said. Jack and I were visiting our kids who lived in Mexico, and I don't speak Spanish.

Sometimes I desperately wish I spoke Spanish. And I do desire to speak Spanish. But I have not paid the price in time or diligence to learn how.

We have no such choice when it comes to learning our partner's language of love if we want to have a deep and intimate love relationship within our marriage.

A recent article explains the importance of this decision: "People fall in love; but they do not fall into marriage. Marriage involves the will as well as the emotions. Marriages are made. They are made initially by mutual consent and commitment. They still have to be made through the sharing of life and love."[1]

One way to "make a marriage" is by determining to understand your partner's principal language of love so that you can begin to build all the secondary ways to communicate love as well. One man said he felt the first task after the wedding vows was to learn his wife's language—how she primarily expressed love. When he understood this language, then he could begin to accept it, appreciate it, develop it, and learn to express it back.

Dr. Gary Chapman suggests there are five basic love languages: touching, talking (or communicating), serving, giving gifts, and encouraging words.[2]

My guess is that if a person was watched closely for as little as twenty-four hours, that person's love language would be discovered. Who do you know who gives you a hug to greet you, who touches you on the arm to make a point, who "pats" you to express sympathy? That one's main love language is probably *touching*.

Do you have a friend who wants deep, intimate sharing, who will spend quality time over a cup of coffee even in the midst of a hectic schedule? The love language is *talking*—communicating.

Perhaps you know a person who finds great delight in doing things for others. This person insists on cleaning up after a dinner party, mowing a neighbor's lawn, and offering to buy groceries for a shut-in. All of this is *serving*.

Then there is the person who is constantly bringing little gifts; whose mind is always in gear to observe what others need; whose favorite pastime is browsing the garage sales or flea markets to pick up things, not for herself or himself but for others. That person is speaking love by *giving gifts*.

And who doesn't appreciate an encourager? But have you thought of that as being a language of love? The person who thinks to say, "That color is perfect for you," or "I realize that your work is mainly behind the scenes, but I wanted to tell you how much I appreciate it," speaks the language of love in *encouraging words*.

Take a husband whose dominant language is serving, and it takes the form of working many hours each week—often overtime—to support his family. His wife's chief language is talking intimately—communicating—but her husband doesn't have time to do that and doesn't suspect that he needs to. She doesn't comprehend his way of showing love and nags him about working so much. He doesn't fathom her love language either and wonders why she nags him about the time he spends working. Because each fails to understand the other's language, neither feels loved or appreciated.

But when they are understood, each can work to esteem the other's language. The wife can be extravagant in her praise of her husband working so hard and doing other things to take care of her and the children. In turn, he must begin to understand her desperate need for intimacy and depth in communicating and plan to spend quality time listening to her "language."

To Mr. Chapman's five languages, we would add some others. You may have even more to include.

As Jack and I discussed the languages of love, we realized that one primary way Jack hears my love is by my being 100 percent with him. Whenever he feels that I am not quite agreeing with what he's doing or the decision that he thought we'd agreed on, he doesn't feel truly loved. Of course we discuss everything, and of course there are times when we don't agree! But when all the discussions are over, he needs to feel I am really with him in my heart. And when he asks, a bit plaintively, "Honey, are you really with me on this?" I know I haven't communicated my loyalty—and therefore, to him, my love.

On the other hand, one primary way I hear Jack's love is by his acceptance of me. You see, I'm kind of a nut, and I know it. I have an active imagination and sometimes ideas pop into my mind that are, well, let's say far out. But to my remembrance, never once has Jack said, "That's got to be the nuttiest idea you ever came up with!" (He may have thought it, but he's never said it!) I feel his acceptance, which says to me, "I love you" (nutty ideas and all).

When we have learned our partner's language of love, then

we can begin to build the secondary languages into our relation-ship and have many creative, wonderful times doing it. But if we are missing the primary language, our partner may not feel loved in any other way and our efforts will go unnoticed.

We've heard remarks such as:

"My husband is always bringing me flowers or candy. It's like he's buying me off for not spending time with our family."

"I work hard all day and then my wife criticizes me for not being romantic!"

"Why doesn't he hold me more when he doesn't want sex? Doesn't he realize I need more nonsexual physical touching?"

"She's always after me to tell her I love her. It's hard for me to be as verbal as she is, but I do try to keep up with all the things in the house that need attention."

Obviously, there may be much more going on in these situa-tions than understanding the other's language. But that might be the first — and simplest — thing to check out. It may just solve the problem.

It's been said, "Neglect the whole world rather than each other." Neglecting the concerted study of our love languages can be harmful to a relationship.

I wonder how many of us know our own language of love? I don't think Jack and I were even aware of how many different lan-guages there were until we analyzed them, and even then some time passed before we realized what ours were.

Besides my primary language of acceptance, I probably speak and hear love in three other dialects! High on my list is a great need for deep, intimate sharing, or in Dr. Chapman's list, "talking."

We should note here that our language reveals itself not only with a marriage partner, but also in the type of sharing we want with others. One wife said, "I like intimate groups where we can share deeply." And her husband countered, "I like large groups where we don't have to share too deeply."[3]

Two of my other top languages are not so significant on Jack's list. I speak love through words—the ever important "I love you," and terms of affection as well as compliments—and through touch and tenderness. I like to hear it that way, too.

Jack, on the other hand, is what could be called a caregiver. One of the ways Jack shows love is by doing things that protect and watch out for me. He tries to think ahead and anticipate what I am going to need.

Probably another strong way Jack hears and gives love is by companionship. He likes us to do things together (and I do too)—to be together—from reading and watching television to traveling and playing golf.

Several years ago Jack did everything but stand on his head to encourage me to learn to play golf. I finally got the message. He didn't care if I was terrible at golf, which I am. He wanted my companionship.

A number of wives ought to check this one out. Some husbands don't seem to care whether their wife shares in their favorite hobby or sport. But others, if companionship is a strong love language, need a wife who will make that extra effort to join them in recreation.

So how do you say "I love you"? How does your spouse say it? If you aren't sure, study your spouse this week with intensity and see if you can discover it.

On your next date, ask each other about the primary way each of you feels love, expresses love. Then ask for opinions on how each of you perceives that the other expresses it and hears it.

I'll guarantee an interesting conversation. And a valuable one.

Notes
1. Joyce Huggett, "A Promise to Love," *Decision* (July-August 1982).
2. The idea is taken from a cassette tape of Gary Chapman, Focus on the Family Ministries.
3. Chuck and Barb Snyder, *Incompatibility: Grounds for a Great Marriage* (Sisters, Oreg.: Questar Publishers, 1988), p. 30.

CHAPTER SEVENTEEN

CHOOSING THE HIGHEST

by Jack

The year before Carole and I were married, we were separated by 300 miles. Both of us were busy. In my last year of college, besides my studies, I was a class officer and involved in athletics. Carole was working twelve to fourteen hours a day as a Christian Education Director. We had agreed that we would write to each other every day. And we kept that agreement.

So every day I would go to my post office box on the college campus, look in, and sure enough, there would be a letter from Carole (and two on Monday).

Well, I found that I was so busy running about the campus that I didn't have time to read her letters each day. So I worked out a little scheme. I would save two or two-and-a-half hours every Sunday afternoon for letter reading time. On Monday, I would go to the post office, get her letters, smell them, and then run off to class. That night I would put her letters on my desk and concentrate on my studies. On Tuesday, Wednesday, Thursday, Friday, and Saturday I'd stack up those letters in the order in which they arrived. Then on Sunday afternoon I would look forward to sitting down, slitting each one open very carefully, and reading them all through, pondering over them till the time would be up and I'd have to get going again.

After we were married, we found ourselves still on a very busy schedule. While at seminary, we lived in a twenty-seven-foot by eight-foot trailer with a concrete path (to the bath, that is). Carole worked to help me through school, and besides studying I worked part time. We found it difficult to coordinate our schedules in such a way that we could stay in touch on a daily basis with everything we wanted to talk about. So we started carrying little notebooks around and from time to time as something came to mind that we wanted to be sure to tell the other, we would jot it down. On Sunday afternoons, we set aside a couple of hours to sit down with our notebooks, and communicate with one another to get caught up on all the things that had happened during the week.

Do you believe me? That isn't what happened at all! We *were* separated and we did agree to write one another every day. But when I went to the mailbox and found that letter, I would rip it open very unceremoniously. I would pull it out, stand right there in the middle of all the mooing herd in the post office area, and I was alone with Carole for the few minutes it took to read her letter. Then if my next class happened to be a particularly dull one, I would read her letter again even if it meant getting caught by the professor. When I got home in the evening, I would take a little time to read the letter more carefully, reading between the lines to figure out what she was really trying to say. We were in love with each other, and this was a love letter from her.

When we were married, we didn't carry little notebooks around to keep track of things. We stayed in touch with one another on a personal basis, and communicated with each other daily.

I use that illustration to point out that there are many Christians in the world who take a strange kind of approach to communicating with God. Their time with Him is relegated to a few minutes each week, perhaps only on Sunday. They set a little time aside on that day, which is the only time they devote to developing communication with God. God has given us the Bible in order to communicate great truths to us, truths He wants us to know regarding Himself, the world, man, and His Son Jesus Christ. But even more than that, He has given us the Bible to tell us things of a personal nature, to get inside our lives and deal with us on specific issues. Many Christians never take enough time to give God an opportunity to speak to them.

Perhaps some of you reading this book consider yourselves to be Christians, those belonging to Christ, those who have invited Jesus Christ to come into their lives to be their Savior. Yet you have never taken the time over a period of months or years to get to know Him. Christ is living in you, He hears your every conversation, He penetrates your thought patterns, and He knows exactly what is going on inside your mind.

We need to get acquainted with Him and let Him talk to us through His Word. An occasional sermon or a Sunday school lesson once a week, while helpful, is not enough. These are like predigested food . . . someone else has gotten the "meat" from the Word of God, chewed it up, savored it, gotten nourishment from it, and then passed it on to us. It can help us, certainly, but such "milk" or "ground up" food is for babies. Growing children and mature adults need solid food, and even babies need to be fed more than once a week. In fact, babies need more feedings per day than adults because they can't take as much in at one time.

So God wants all of us, whether we are newly born into His Kingdom or have been Christians for some time, to begin feeding individually and daily on His Word.

God, our heavenly Father, desires fellowship with us daily because He loves us. He has written us a love letter that He wants us to read so we can get to know Him. He has made available to us this beautiful thing we call prayer, which is our communication link with Him to let Him know what is on our hearts and to talk over with Him our problems, concerns, and things that are bothering us. We share with Him things that make us joyful and happy and that we are thankful for. We have an open channel of communication to Him in prayer and through the Bible.

Many people lose out on really knowing God because their approach to communicating with Him is like my hypothetical story. We read His love letter once a week (perhaps have it read to us in church), and we talk to Him when we get into a jam. But we fail to take advantage of the open access we have to fellowship with Him on a daily basis.

The Lord has said, "To this man will I look, even to him that is poor and of a contrite spirit, and trembleth at my word" (Isaiah 66:2, KJV). Trembles here does not have the sense of being fearful, but trembling in the sense of being respectful and eager to find out what God has to say.

God's statement to Jeremiah has often challenged me:

> Thus says the LORD, "Let not a wise man boast of his wisdom, and let not the mighty man boast of his might, let not a rich man boast of his riches; but let him who boasts boast of this, that he understands and knows Me, that I am the LORD who exercises lovingkindness, justice, and righteousness on earth; for I delight in these things," declares the LORD. (Jeremiah 9:23-24)

God says that if you want to boast about something, it should not be because you are smart or powerful or strong or rich. It should be in the fact that you know Him in an intimate way because God delights in your knowing Him.

The psalmist makes quite a promise when he says, "Great peace have they who love your law, and nothing can make them stumble" (Psalm 119:165, NIV). What a motivation to get into the Word of God and find out what God wants to say to us. Our approach to the Bible should be like listening to a voice rather than reading a book. We should hear His voice saying, "This is your Father speaking. Listen!" If He has taken the trouble to put into writing the thoughts, ideas, and words He wants to communicate to us, He wants to be listened to and obeyed. When God speaks, He means to be taken seriously.

It takes three people to make a lasting marriage: a man, a woman, and God. Our communication link to each other as husband and wife has to be forged stronger as the years go by. Even more vital is our communication link individually with the One who created us both.

How much time can you give out of twenty-four hours to talk with God? You need eight hours for sleep and eight for work, then perhaps two to eat. That leaves about six. What can you give God out of your free six hours each day?

Some can give Him an hour, some thirty minutes, some fifteen. If you have never developed a time to spend each day with God, don't start with any of those larger amounts of time. Try just seven minutes a day to spend all alone in God's presence. Here is how to spend that precious seven minutes.

1. *Half a minute—Pray.*

In that thirty seconds, pray, "Open thou mine eyes, that I may behold wondrous things out of thy law" (Psalm 119:18, KJV). You might say something like, "Now, Lord, I am going to open Your Word in just a minute to read it and see what You have to say to me. I pray that You will open the eyes of my spiritual understanding that I might be able to grasp what it is that You are trying to say to me personally today."

2. *Four minutes—Read God's Word.*

If this is new to you, start with the book of Philippians, which is a warm and intimate book the Apostle Paul wrote to Christian friends. Don't try to read a whole chapter. Take a few verses and read them slowly and thoughtfully. Think about them, and ask, "What is God saying to me from them?"

3. *Two-and-a-half minutes—Pray.*

It may be that God has said something to you which you need to pray over. You may need strength and help to do what He has told you to do. Spend a moment thanking Him and praising Him for being so good to you. Tell Him of the burdens and problems that are uppermost in your mind. Pray through your day, appointments, situations, meetings, and problems you might be facing.[1]

In order to do this effectively, you are obviously going to need to find a time and a place. If we are going to fellowship with God, we need to give Him the best part of the day. He deserves that. The time will be different for various individuals. For some, the best part of the day is in the morning. Some "night people" will be most alert in the evening. For a busy mother, it might be the children's naptime; for a businessman, lunch time could be best.

But find a time when it is quiet for your time alone with God.

If you will do this consistently for four weeks, I will give you an iron-clad guarantee. I will guarantee you that you will begin noticing a difference in your own life. Changes of attitude will begin to take place; you will become more sensitive to sin in your life.

Next, your mate will begin to notice these changes. You will be a nicer person to live with, a more enjoyable individual to be around, because God will begin to change things in your life that will make a difference in your marriage relationship.

Paul states categorically that "all scripture is given by inspiration of God, and is profitable for doctrine, for reproof, for correction, for instruction in righteousness" (2 Timothy 3:16, KJV).

- *For doctrine*—so that we might know the great truths that are revealed in the Word of God.
- *For reproof*—so that we might hear God's rebukes and reprimands concerning our sins and manner of life.
- *For correction*—so that we might change and rectify our behavior when He has reproved us.
- *For instruction in righteousness*—so that we might live the kind of life that reflects Jesus Christ consistently.

Paul then gives us the reason: "that the man [or woman] of God may be adequate [or perfect, mature, growing toward maturity], equipped for every good work" (3:17). That is fantastic. God does not say we have to have a college degree, go to a certain kind of church, or have unique gifts and abilities. He says that if we are faithful to get into the Word, it will be profitable in four ways and the result of that will be Christian maturity.

And His Word will equip us to serve God in whatever way He wants us to serve Him.

Take me up on my guarantee today, for "today is the first day of the rest of your life!" Use it to communicate with God and strengthen your marriage.

Note

1. A longer explanation of this quiet time with God may be found in the pamphlet by Robert D. Foster, *Seven Minutes with God*, obtainable from your local Christian bookstore.

CHAPTER EIGHTEEN

CHOOSING SOME "NEVERS"

by Jack

Carole and I were sitting in a motel dining room having breakfast when we became aware of a conversation near us. A couple was discussing finances and the man had just told his wife of some investment plans he was considering.

Suddenly the woman's strident voice rose above the noise of the diners as she exclaimed, "And where do you think you are going to get that kind of money? What are you going to do, sell my underwear?"

All eyes turned toward the pair. The man flushed, looked down, and never spoke a word.

It was the ultimate sarcastic remark—a cut-down that was a perfect put-down. Obviously, she had grown quite adept with her verbal rapier.

Momentarily I wondered if Carole and I could have ever grown so proficient. I thank God that He detoured us from that muddy road years ago.

Some things Carole and I simply never do. I often refer to these as the "nevers" in our relationship, because we have learned that for a couple they spell disaster.

The number one never for us is: never use sarcasm in conversing with one another.

The dictionary defines sarcasm as, "A sharp and often satiri-cal or ironic utterance designed to cut or give pain . . . a mode of satirical wit depending for its effect on bitter, caustic, and often ironic language that is usually directed against an individual." It comes from a Greek word meaning "to tear flesh, bite the lips in rage, sneer."[1] A perfect illustration is the woman's remark con-cerning the selling of her underwear.

In American culture, we have become adept at the sarcastic remark. Many TV situation comedies are based on it. Don Rickles has made a fortune from it. But in marital relationships it is a "never" for Carole and me.

This was not always true. Shortly after we were married, we discovered that we had developed an ingrained habit of the sar-castic joke in kidding one another. At first, as we made little barbs and sharp remarks, they were totally harmless. We meant noth-ing by them. But over a period of a couple of years, we began to discover that this habit had become a convenient way of getting in a good dig at the other partner every now and then. The other person did not know whether it was to be taken seriously or not. We could hint at a truth in our sarcasm that we were afraid to share honestly; and the other, not knowing if the intent was seri-ous, was unable to take offense. We discovered that we were hurt-ing one another.

One summer, about two years after we were married, we worked with a pastor and his wife and spent many hours with them. It was obvious to us that this older couple was deeply in love and had a great time together. Gradually we began to notice that in all the hours we spent with them, we never heard them resort to sarcasm as a means of joking or kidding one another. Halfway through the summer, we asked them about it. Interest-ingly, they related our own story back to us. They had also found themselves hurting each other by sarcasm after they were married and found it convenient to use a sharp barb when they didn't like something in the other partner. When they recognized what they were doing and the hurt it was causing, they prayed about it together and covenanted with each other to stop doing it. It took some time because it had become an unconscious habit, but finally they conquered it with the help of the Lord. They shared with us what a great difference it had made in their marital relationship.

Following their example, Carole and I did the same thing. We prayed about it, confessed it as sin, and covenanted with one another to drop it from our lives. It took a few weeks even to get to the place where we were conscious when we did it, as by then to come back with a nasty crack was almost automatic, but finally we eliminated it from our kidding vocabulary.

Couples, even whole families, commonly make the ones they love the brunt of a put-down. Some are totally unaware of the shadow of hurt on the other's face as the barb finds its mark. As we entered a church where we were to have a weekend seminar on the marriage relationship, we met the pastor. As he was introduced to us, he quipped sarcastically, "Well, I'm sure going to pay my wife's way for this one!" He had become adept at the barb game.

A second never for us is: never criticize or correct one another in public.

A husband and wife are leaving a party, and he says to the host, "Thanks for inviting us over. It's such a welcome change from TV dinners." Funny? Maybe. Kind? No.

Or the husband says to the man who is giving him some directions, "You'd better tell me. Jeannie could get lost with a police escort." Funny? Maybe. Kind? No.[2]

This sort of remark not only is unkind, but it makes one's mate look small. Do we really want our spouses to look small in the eyes of other people? We need to love more than that.

Many things we do cause others to look small in the eyes of friends. Sometimes a wife asks her husband to tell his favorite story at a gathering of friends. She has coaxed him, knows it is a favorite of his, and he loves to tell it. So he begins his story. He gets into it and leaves something out. So she says, "Oh, honey, you left out the part about . . . ," and he backs up and puts in that detail.

As he goes into another section of the story and changes a percentage, she corrects him. In another part he adds a statement that she has not heard before, so she sets him straight. (After all, it is his story; he should be able to tell it like he wants to, with any changes he pleases.)

After the fourth correction in front of his friends, he finally explodes, "Oh, you tell it!"

Why do we think it is our God-given right or responsibility to correct our mates anywhere, under any conditions, no matter what? It is a tragic habit with terrible consequences. It throws water on the fire of spontaneity and love.

Sarcasm, criticism, and correcting are simply not *kind*. And to love a person is to practice steadfastly God's admonition for us to be kind one to another (see Ephesians 4:32).

Notes

1. By permission. From *Webster's New Collegiate Dictionary*. © 1977 by G. & C. Merriam Co., Publishers of the Merriam-Webster Dictionaries, p. 1025.

2. Adapted from Charlie Shedd, *Letters to Philip* (Garden City, N.Y.: Doubleday and Company, Inc., 1968), p. 60.

CHAPTER NINETEEN

CHOOSING TO PAY THE PRICE

by Jack and Carole

JACK

He was a very busy man; his wife felt that he was too busy. It had been some time since they had spent some private time together in his crowded schedule. So when she came across his appointment book one day, she wrote in her own name for "12:00 lunch on Tuesday" and didn't say a word to him.

A couple of days later she looked on his Tuesday calendar and found that her name had been neatly crossed out and a business appointment written in. Her husband hadn't said a word to her either.

The wife tells this story with a rueful smile. It's a wonder that she can still manage that.

We have a price to pay for depth in sharing in another's life. And the one payment that will yield the greatest interest is time together. And one of the most valuable means of keeping in touch with another's heart is to play "The Dating Game" regularly.

Carole and I started dating decades ago and we intend to keep on dating till we can't hobble out the door any longer. Our goal is to have a date once a week, though we don't always achieve our aim. To get away from the house, the phone, the mad jumble of things, and to get alone is the point. We may have a candlelight dinner at our favorite restaurant or just a McDonald's hamburger or a pizza. Where we go is relatively unimportant. Going is the major thing.

The purpose for going out on a date is to talk. We want to get caught up with one another's inner thoughts and heartbeat. We find in these times that we get into subjects that we don't think to talk about in our busy days at home when interruptions are frequent. Our kind of date doesn't need to cost much, or cost anything at all. A drive to a favorite park, a picnic, a bicycle ride on a spring day. In our graduate school days, when money was nonexistent, we would go to a large department store, seclude ourselves in a little private record booth, and play all the newest records. When we could really splurge, we would even buy a forty-five-rpm record for about fifty cents.

Dates don't have to be costly, but the price must be paid in discipline and in time — the discipline of making it a priority, of saying no to some other projects, the discipline of taking the time.

Another thing Carole and I do is trade off with one another in planning dates. It's a lot of fun. The husband plans things he knows his wife enjoys (window shopping? picnics?), while the wife reciprocates (golfing? mountain climbing?). The idea of a date is to get time alone together. Our double dating stopped after college. I don't mean that we no longer go out with other couples, but that time doesn't count as our date. When the children are little and money is scarce, dating takes more doing. Trading off with the neighbors on the babysitting part may work; it will be well worth the trouble, and we feel it is a big factor in keeping the romance and sparkle in any relationship.

But once a week dating isn't enough. Another goal every couple should aim for is a few minutes each day to stay in touch.

Over the years, we have had to do this at different times because of our changing schedules and circumstances — our daughter growing up, people living in our home, changes in work responsibilities. Now that we are alone, we do it at breakfast. In the last several years, when we've had people living in our home, we'd wait till they had to leave for work and then sit down together. We would take twenty or thirty minutes to linger over a third cup of coffee and talk. Occasionally I have a breakfast meeting, but as much as possible we consider breakfast as our time. We guard it jealously because we need it to stay in touch with one another and to continue forging the links of our lives together.

One more time-commitment needed is the time to become, not just friends, but *companions.*

Dr. Willard F. Harley, Jr., a licensed clinical psychologist and author of *His Needs, Her Needs: Building an Affair-Proof Marriage,* commented:

> I define a need as what people enjoy tremendously
> when someone does that for them. I've discovered that in
> women, the primary needs are: affection, conversation,
> honesty and openness (a solid basis of trust), financial sup-
> port (enough money to live comfortably), and family com-
> mitment (her husband must be a good father).
>
> Among men, the five basics needs are: sexual fulfill-
> ment, recreational companionship (having his wife join
> him in leisure activities), an attractive spouse (she tries to
> always look her best), domestic support (he finds peace
> and quiet at home), and admiration.[2]

Interesting that the second requisite in men, according to Dr. Harley, is "recreational companionship."

Dr. Lois Leiderman Davitz underscores this desire in an article concerning why men divorce. Four hundred divorced men between the ages of twenty and forty-five were asked why they thought their marriages disintegrated. Money (mentioned by 5 percent), sex (49 percent said sexual problems con-tributed), and child-rearing (42 percent) came in for a share, of course. But what virtually every man in her study cited as decisive in the failure of the relationship was lack of companionship. Universally, these men felt that their marriage fell apart because they stopped being friends with their wives.

Dr. Davitz went on to say,

> Companionship has a very special meaning for men. A companion is someone with whom you share activities that you enjoy. Almost all of these failed marriages, as reported by the men, involved very few shared activities. . . . Almost without exception, the men talked about their longing for a wife who would be a friend. "I wanted my ex to do things with me, show an interest in what I liked doing," says Larry, 36. "She hated my motor-cycle and accused me of using it as an escape to be with my buddies. I'd like her to know that my current girlfriend has her own Honda."
>
> The men were equally clear about what companion-ship is not. It's not sex, though a desire for sex may grow out of companionship. It's not parallel activities, such as sitting together and watching TV. It's not necessarily out-ings with the children. Many men complained that all their recreation with their wives involved the entire family.[3]

A great many wives have never seriously thought about what constitutes companionship, or even friendship, for their husband or how he defines communication. Often she makes friends on the basis of commonality of feelings while he makes friends on the basis of commonality of activities. (Note Dr. Davitz's definition of a companion being "someone with whom you share activities that you enjoy.") His best buddy will be his business partner or the man he plays tennis with on weekends.

Communication to her involves sharing hearts. Communica-tion to him involves discussing what has been done together.

Because of this, one counselor suggests that when things seem to be getting rocky, a woman needs to make an extra effort to do things with her husband. He says to try to include an activity each day that you both enjoy and carve out time to share it with him.

And laugh together! The divorced men who were interviewed consistently reported that they had fun with their wives less than once a month.[4]

Because some wives fail to understand how their husbands make and view friends, they don't see the importance of learning to enjoy what their husbands enjoy. Some say, "I can't." Others say, "Why should I?" Still others say, "What difference does it make?"

I think Dr. Harley and Dr. Davitz give us answers to the last two. And God gives us the answer to the first.

CAROLE

I often wonder if women who say "I can't" have ever really made it a matter of prayer. I cling to the fact that our God will never give us a command that He won't give us the ability to carry out! And it isn't our husbands who say, "Adapt to your husband" (Ephesians 5:22, PH—one meaning of the Greek word for "submit"). It is God.

I am convinced that God has given women a unique ability to adapt, to change. But we rarely ask Him for His help in this area.

I have to tell you, I prayed a lot about graduating from spectator to participant in sports. I don't like to be humiliated any more than anyone else! (And still I have to say to myself, "Carole, your self-worth is not bound up in how you play golf!"—because if it were, I wouldn't have any!)

When Jack and I first realized that one of the weakest areas of our marriage was recreational intimacy, we explored sports that we might play together and decided on tennis. Jack had played tennis in high school; I'd never owned a racket.

I had to pray for two things: (1) that I'd like it—because I knew I'd never pursue it if I hated it, (2) that I'd have enough ability not to disgrace us both.

God answered. I loved it! And by taking lessons and practicing, I got so I could play a pretty good game of mixed doubles with Jack—and it added a new interest for us so that we both enjoyed watching professional tennis as well.

Then Jack injured his knee—weak from an old skiing accident—and he couldn't play tennis anymore.

It was at that point, I took up golf. I had to ask the Lord for the same two things, and God has answered—well, at least the first one.

If He can do it for me, wives, He can do it for you!

So keep learning. Keep growing. I feel that some new interest—not previously explored—should be added to our lives every few years. It can be a hobby, a course taken together, a sport, a board game, a new outreach such as teaching a Sunday school class together.

Obviously, this is a two-way street. A husband should learn to enjoy what his wife enjoys as well. Both partners should work at stretching their horizons.

I have to admit there are some things I'd have a harder time adjusting to than others. I'm glad Jack doesn't hunt. And I'm glad he doesn't like to watch wrestling. (Whew!)

But I am convinced should he enjoy even those, God could help me like them. After all, God made me to be Jack's wife and therefore can help each of us "fit."

For deep and growing communication, the price is paid in time. It takes time to enjoy one another on dates. It takes disciplined periods sectioned from our lives each day to explore our hearts fully. And it takes a multitude of fragments snatched from the minutes of each day that ensure depth of meaning in our lives together.

Notes
1. Annie Gottlieb, "The Heart of Every Successful Marriage," *Reader's Digest* (April 1988), p. 33.
2. "Building An Affair-Proof Marriage," interview with Dr. Willard F. Harley, *Contact* (June-July 1987), p. 15.
3. Lois Leiderman Davitz, "Why Men Divorce," *The Colorado Springs Gazette Telegraph* (April 7, 1987).
4. Davitz, "Why Men Divorce."

CHAPTER TWENTY

CHOOSING
TO OVERLOOK

by Jack

We were running fifteen minutes late and were rushing to get dressed for an important dinner when it happened for the tenth time that week. Carole and I arrived at our "closet-with-the-sliding-door" at precisely the same instant. For a second we stood staring at each other. Then we burst into laughter, and I bowed in exaggerated jest, motioning her to go ahead and get her things out first. With a sliding door closet, only one part can be opened at a time.

I had not always been able to laugh. I had gone through occasions when my thoughts had grumbled and then flared, "Why does she always have to get into the closet when I need to?"

On such trivial matters, marriages hang together or fall apart.

Carole and I have been in the school of learning daily relationships ever since we met. We went together for three-and-a-half years on the same college campus and the pressure this caused was acute. I am a perfectionist and over the months a number of Carole's habits and mannerisms began to irk me. Simultaneously, little things I would say or do bothered her. These things piled up over a period of weeks till one final item would start the "can you top this?" game of irritation sharing. Two or three days would be spent in resolving our problems.

When this had happened several times, we realized we had a problem which we could not handle, and decided to ask the advice of Dr. Brooks, a godly dean at our college. He listened to our story, smiled knowingly, and gave us some of the best advice we've ever had. He said, "Mrs. Brooks and I have been married over 30 years. If we had let the little things that irritated us about one another build up, we would probably have been divorced years ago. But early in our marriage we learned that we had to forgive and forget, to overlook and make allowances for, and accept each other for what we were. Some things needed to be talked about and solutions found, but things that couldn't be changed must be forgiven immediately and forgotten."

That was so practical. So when a little thing began to fester, we immediately exposed it, discussed it, and decided together what could be changed. When I told Carole that the bobby pins she wore in her hair poked me in the cheek when she put her head on my shoulder, she changed her hairstyle and has never worn bobby pins since. No big deal. And she helped me correct sentences in which I was using incorrect grammar.

But the things that couldn't be changed, such as the inability to play golf well, to think with complete logic, to feel intuitively when one is depressed, to tell a joke so that the punch line comes out right, we asked God for the ability to forgive, forget, and accept about each other.

In the early years together, irritations can literally bombard a couple. Men who leave socks in the middle of the bedroom, don't hang up their pajamas, and leave globs of toothpaste in the bathroom marry neat, precise women who snatch a newspaper away before the husband is finished reading it to put it away in its proper place.

We've certainly had our share. I have to laugh in retrospect at all the lessons we learned through that one "closet-with-the-slid-ing-door." At times when we didn't arrive at the closet at the same moment, I would try to open my side, only to have the door stop short. Looking in on Carole's side, I would see a nice neat row of three pairs of shoes that weren't quite in the closet. That would irk me to no end. I would think, Why in the world can't Carole put her shoes all the way into the closet? So I would kick them in.

Sometimes I would reach into the shower stall to turn on the water and instead of a nice, bright, shiny cold faucet, I would touch a soggy washcloth draped over the faucet. What a terrible way to begin a shower!

These irritations need to be talked about. Those that cannot be changed, such as arriving at the closet door simultaneously, need to be treated with humor, forgiven, and forgotten.

One thing I still cannot figure out. How is it that I can take off two socks, dutifully put them in the dirty clothes hamper, have them go through the washing and drying process, and have only one sock get back into my drawer? We must have a washer that eats socks. Carole has even solved this irritation. She simply does not put one sock back anymore till the other one shows up. Of course I have to have a little larger inventory of socks that way!

These are all funny, stupid, frustrating, and trivial matters of our existence. Yet so many relationships are destroyed over them. But our God is in control over even the funny, stupid, frustrating, and trivial matters. He is not only in the business of changing people, but He can help us be creative in our solutions for changing the habits of our lives. He has helped me learn to hang up a bath towel with the monogram right side out and precisely centered. I don't leave my pajamas in the center of the bedroom any more (I pile them in a neat little stack by the wall now). Carole doesn't hang the washcloth over the shower faucet but on an added towel rack.

We are learning, with God's help, to adjust, to change, and to accept. And we have discovered that even that can be fun.

CHAPTER TWENTY-ONE

CHOOSING TO FOLLOW THE WAY

by Carole

After an afternoon at the county fair, two country boys discovered they each had only a quarter left. One decided to ride the merry-go-round, but the other declined. When the first boy finished his ride, he asked his friend why he hadn't ridden with him. The second boy replied, "Well, you spent all your money, you got off where you got on, and you ain't been nowhere."

How many of us feel something of the same? We look back on some days and think, *We've spent all our money, we got off where we got on, and we ain't been nowhere.*

God would not have it so. He wants each of us to be somebody, to go somewhere, and to have a life that is full of meaning and purpose.

How is this possible?

We had lived in the Chicago area a number of years when a friend invited me to have lunch with her at the Deerpath Inn in a northern suburb. (Just how far north it was I was to discover later.) She had given me directions from my home in a northeastern suburb, but I started out from a location nearer to Lake Michigan. Somehow I had it fixed in my mind that Deerpath Inn was in Deerfield. My logic centered in the fact they both began with "deer." Actually, the restaurant is in Lake Bluff, a few suburbs north of Deerfield.

I thought I knew a quicker route to Deerfield than she had given me, so I started up a main diagonal road. I drove and drove and drove and couldn't find Illinois Road, where she had directed me to turn. By this time I was late and a bit frantic. So I did what women will do and men seem to have a hard time doing . . . I got off the road and went into a filling station to ask for some directions.

I looked at the attendant hopelessly and said, "Please, can you help me? I'm lost."

He asked, "Where are you going?"

"Deerpath Inn," I responded.

"Oh, okay," he replied and scratched his head. "Let's see, you go one block north and three blocks east . . . no, that's not so good. Go three blocks north and two blocks east . . . well, perhaps a better way is for you to go. . . ."

He told me three different ways to go, and by this time I was utterly confused.

A nicely dressed gentleman was in the station at the time, standing there and taking it all in. Finally, he turned to me and said, "Would you like to follow me to your destination?"

I thought, Whew! Would I!

The attendant asked him if he was going to Deerpath Inn, and the man replied, "No, but I live in Lake Bluff and will be going right past it. I would be happy to show this lady the way."

So I said, "Thank you so much," and he got in his car and I in mine and we started out in an entirely different direction than the three ways the station attendant had suggested. We drove on the tiniest, squiggliest, awfullest, backest roads you ever saw in your life. And you can imagine what was going through my mind all this time. Where is he taking me? What is he going to do when he gets me there? I was so horribly lost that I felt committed to wherever he was taking me.

It seemed like an eternity, but I'm sure it was just a few short minutes till we turned on to Illinois Road and pulled up in front of the Deerpath Inn. This man was even so kind as to get out of his car, come back to mine, and bend down to ask through my window, "Now do you think you can find your way back?"

I smiled, and assured him that my friend would help me.

I couldn't help thinking afterward that this experience was an interesting parallel to life.

Most of us start out on our journey of life fairly confident that we know where we are going and how we are going to get there. Of course in my generation the goal for many women was to "get married and live happily ever after" (a very short-range and unrealistic goal for sure). We think we have the necessary knowledge of direction and purpose in life.

And so we begin. We go till something makes us realize that we aren't getting anywhere. An empty marriage, a child that isn't turning out the way we hoped, an illness, a death, financial reverses . . . or maybe just a hollow feeling deep down inside that tells us there has to be more to life than we are experiencing. Something makes us realize that we are lost.

We begin by searching for the way to fulfillment, but we obtain confusing directions. One person tells us that a career will fulfill us. We may believe that till we read a quote from *Family Weekly* by Taylor Caldwell, well-known author. She was asked if the nine-hour TV production of her book *Captains and Kings* brought her the solid satisfaction that seemed denied her by Hollywood's failure to make films of her previous books. Her answer was heartbreaking:

> There is no solid satisfaction in any career for a woman like myself. There is no home, no true freedom, no hope, no joy, no expectation for tomorrow, no contentment. I would rather cook a meal for a man and bring him his slippers and feel myself in the protection of his arms than have all the citations and awards and honors I have

received worldwide, including the Ribbon of Legion of Honor and my property and my bank accounts. They mean nothing to me. And I am only one among the millions of sad women like myself.[1]

Another person tells us that our fulfillment comes in quality education. We listen to others telling us to immerse ourselves in our families in order to fulfill our lives. Some say enrichment comes through power or money. But as we try these methods and directions, nothing seems to fill that vacuum which keeps telling us we haven't yet found the answer.

At some point in our lives we are confronted with the One who looks at us tenderly and asks, "Would you like to follow Me?"

This Person looks as though He could be the Way . . . and someone else may have told you that He is, but each individual has to make the decision as to whether to believe Him and accept His credentials. I am speaking, of course, of Jesus Christ. He made some astounding claims. He claimed to be God . . . and He had to be in order to be the Way for us. He claimed to have the power to forgive sins, to give us not only eternal life in the future but a new quality of life here and now (John 10:10).

You see, we have not only lost the way to a fulfilling life, but the reason we don't have a fulfilling life is because we are lost to God Himself. We are lost . . . separated from God by our rebellion against Him, by insisting on going on our own way, and by all the things that are wrong with our lives. As a just and holy God, He has to judge these sins. God stands in front of me, as it were, and reads off all the things that are wrong with me, and the list is quite long. He would say to me, "Carole, you are a selfish, willful, proud, jealous, and angry person," and on and on He could go. In all honesty I would have to admit, "Yes, Lord, You are absolutely right!" And God being God has to judge and exact payment.

But then Jesus Christ steps forward and says, "But remember, Father, I have already borne the penalty of all those sins Carole has committed. I came down to earth . . . lived a perfect life . . . and met all Your requirements for righteousness, so that there is no need for Carole to pay the consequences of sin, which are death and separation from You. And I chose to give My life on the cross . . . and I did it for Carole and for all who have sinned." (See Romans 3:23, 6:23.)

Then the Father says, "Of course, I remember." He now turns to me and asks, "What are you going to do about it? Do you accept the sacrifice of My Son?"

I have a choice to make. I can say, "Thank You, Lord Jesus, I accept Your sacrifice. Thank You for taking my penalty on Yourself by dying for me. I accept You as my Savior and Lord." And at that moment I am cleansed from all my sins and become a child of God. I am born into the family of God and become a "Christ-one" or Christian.

Or I can say, "Thank You, but I'll try to do it my own way." If I respond this way, Christ looks sadly at me and says, "Carole, there is no other way. I am the Way, the Truth, and the Life. No one can come to the Father except through Me." (See John 14:6.)

If I reject His offer, I continue to be spiritually dead . . . lost to God and lost to being a fulfilled person.

Jesus Christ is our only way to life without end . . . to a dimension in our lives and relationships that will be rich with meaning and love. He is the source of love, of joy, of peace. When you have Him—when you say yes to His invitation to follow Him and ask Him to be your Savior and Lord—never again will you feel that you have been on a merry-go-round heading nowhere.

Note
1. Taylor Caldwell, "Ask Them Yourself," *Family Weekly*, September 19, 1976. Reprint by permission of *FAMILY WEEKLY*, copyright © 1976, 641 Lexington Avenue, New York, NY 10022.

PART FOUR

WHAT IS INVOLVED IN LOVE?

CHAPTER TWENTY-TWO

CHOOSING TO OBEY GOD

by Jack

It was a nightmare and I wanted desperately to pinch myself awake. Only pinching didn't help because it was real.

I had been speaking at a conference outside a small village in The Netherlands. Having an afternoon to myself, I borrowed a car to go into town for some shopping. The "small village" turned out to be a thriving little city with streets going off in all directions. Apparently in turning off the main road, I had lost my sense of direction and found myself hopelessly lost.

It is one thing to be lost in a country where you know the language. It is another to be surrounded by people with whom you can't converse.

I was greatly relieved when I finally found a kind, English-speaking hotel clerk who offered to help me. But when I started to ask directions back to the conference grounds, I suddenly realized that I didn't know the name of the conference center, nor the road on which it was located. And everyone I knew in Holland who might know was already at the conference.

I stared at the clerk in consternation. What a predicament to be in! Finally, after quite some time of telephoning all possible conference facilities within a radius of twenty miles, my benefactor located the place from which I was lost.

At times, we are unaware of having lost our sense of direction. Later, however, there is a growing realization we are lost, when we can't discover any clues to familiar ground.

Many Christian husbands today are "lost" in an area of their marriages and don't even know it. When they discover they have been traveling a wrong road, they don't know where to begin to get "found" again.

Some men don't even care that they are heading in the wrong direction. Some are actually deluded into thinking that they are doing right and pleasing God, even while they are disobeying some of His commands.

The particular command—which some ignore, many do not understand, and most can't do—is given to us three times within a single paragraph by the Apostle Paul. It is the command to love your wife (Ephesians 5:25,28,33).

"Nonsense," you might respond. "I love my wife. I wouldn't have married her otherwise."

But do you? Do you love her in the way God commands you to love her?

In a home that is dedicated to serving Christ, all the family members give of themselves, their time, and their energies to bringing men and women to Jesus and to helping them grow into productive disciples. The husband in this household truly "denies himself"—in terms of time, energy, relaxation. But unconsciously perhaps, he may feel that because he and his wife are "one," it is all right for him to deny her his time, energy, and times for relaxation as well.

Paul wrote:

Husbands, love your wives, just as Christ also loved the church and gave Himself up for her; that He might sanctify her, having cleansed her by the washing of water with the word, that He might present to Himself the church in all her glory, having no spot or wrinkle or any such thing; but that she should be holy and blameless. So husbands ought also to love their own wives as their own bodies. He who loves his own wife loves himself; for no one ever hated his own flesh, but nourishes and cherishes it, just as Christ also does the church, because we are members of His body. FOR THIS CAUSE A MAN SHALL LEAVE HIS FATHER AND MOTHER, AND SHALL CLEAVE TO HIS WIFE, AND THE TWO SHALL BECOME ONE FLESH. This mystery is great; but I am speaking with reference to Christ and the church. Nevertheless let each individual among you also love his own wife even as himself; and let the wife see to it that she respect her husband. (Ephesians 5:25-33)

According to the Word of God, the husband is commanded to love his wife in an extraordinary manner. He is to love her in the same way that Christ loves the Church, as he does his own body, and as he loves himself. That is one tall order!

Throughout the New Testament, we as Christians are commanded to love one another. But this is the only place in all of the Bible where one person is commanded to love another in the same way as Christ loves the Church. God ordained this relationship to exist between a husband and a wife. It is uniquely different from any other in all of His creation.

Tragically, some men have a more unique relationship with their set of golf clubs. Or the ministry in which they are involved. Or even with their children. Somehow many wives come out as the lowest person on the totem pole.

John said, "Let us not love with word or with tongue, but in deed and truth" (1 John 3:18). A man who denies his wife his own self, his energy, his time, and his thought does not love his wife in deed (by his actions) nor in truth. Neither does he love her the way Christ loved the Church—which was and is totally giving of Himself.

Love and admiration are necessary both for a husband and wife. But to be loved is more important for a woman, while admiration is significant to a man.

It is important that a woman know she is loved. And that love has to be communicated in such a way that she feels it. Love has to be manifested in terms of words and actions.

The epitome of love is expressed best in what has been called the "Love Chapter" in the Bible. Notice the descriptive words that denote action in this passage:

> Love is very patient and kind, never jealous or envious,
> never boastful or proud, never haughty or selfish or rude.
> Love does not demand its own way. It is not irritable or
> touchy. It does not hold grudges and will hardly even
> notice when others do it wrong. It is never glad about
> injustice, but rejoices whenever truth wins out. If you love
> someone you will be loyal to him no matter what the cost.
> You will always believe in him, always expect the best of
> him, and always stand your ground in defending him.
> (1 Corinthians 13:4-7, TLB)

From time to time it would be a good idea for all of us who are married to read this passage together while holding hands, then make a fresh commitment in asking God for this kind of love for one another.

When God speaks, He means to be taken seriously. When He tells husbands to love their wives, not once, but three times in one passage, it must be important to God that men do it. The major question, of course, is how?

In order to communicate to Carole that I love her, I try to do three things every single day. I don't always reach this goal, but I try.

The first is to tell her that I love her.

A cartoon showed a wife asking her husband over and over, "Do you love me?" He would not answer her till, in exasperation in the last frame, he shouted, "Of course I love you. That's my job!"

The man was certainly right. It is our job. But somehow I don't think his answer satisfied his wife.

One man got so tired of hearing his wife ask him if he loved her day after day that he went into his workshop and engraved a little wooden plaque with the words "I love you." He then took it to the kitchen, hung it over the sink, and brought his wife in to see it. "There," he said triumphantly, "I have said it! It's in writing! Now let's forget it!" I don't believe his answer satisfied his wife either.

That approach simply won't work. A wife needs to hear that she is loved and hear it often. It doesn't have to be a romantic setting all the time. A quick "I love you" as you walk out the door, another as she's cooking supper, or a small hug and a whisper as you pass each other in the hall will do wonders.

I aim every day to tell Carole that I love her.

My second goal is to do something nice for her each day.

This one is more difficult. It takes considerable creativity and thought. Dawson Trotman, founder of The Navigators, said many times, "Think—there is so little competition."

Many wives, subconsciously or consciously, think of their homes as an extension of their personalities, especially if the wife is not working outside the home. As she has more time to give to her home, the rooms begin to reflect the kind of person she is. Husbands would do well to remember that. When a husband neglects those little things around the home that she has asked him to do—in fact sometimes nagged him to do—she takes it personally. It speaks to her in terms of love. If she is thinking of her home as an extension of herself, then when her husband neglects it, he neglects her. Men rarely see it that way. Little jobs around the house are twentieth down on their priority lists.

For you to demonstrate your love for your wife, you must try to see things from her point of view. What does your wife enjoy doing that doesn't take much effort but at the same time would please her? Carole enjoys window-shopping at an enclosed shopping center near our home. On the other hand, walking around on the hard cement and staring in glass windows is not exactly my idea of having a good time. Yet I know she enjoys it. And I enjoy being with her. So, on occasion, I try to get home a little early from work and suggest that we go and do some window-shopping. It takes a little time, a little energy, a little sacrifice, a little initiative on my part, but it is well worth it. It is a way I can tell her that I care, that I love her.

Another idea is to send your wife a three-word telegram sometime when you are out of town. Just say, "I LOVE YOU," and leave it unsigned.

When was the last time you brought your wife some flowers? Not for any special occasion, such as a birthday, but just because you love her? Most men have no idea of the meaning of flowers to a woman. We are inclined to think, *Will they last? Will they be useful?* To many women, the very fact that they aren't practical and won't last gives her a special sense of feeling loved just for herself alone.

Sometime when you have to leave early for a breakfast appointment and you are being very quiet so she can sleep in a bit, surprise her with a message on the mirror or tile (written with easily removed soap or eyebrow pencil, please), scrawled in your handwriting, "I love you."

Express your love by doing something nice for her every day. After one marriage seminar Carole and I held, one man's wife was thrilled because he let her out at the church door instead of making her walk from the parking lot. She'd wanted him to do that for her, but for twelve years he stubbornly refused. These are little things, but they speak volumes to a woman's heart.

The third thing I try to do every day is to pay Carole a compliment.

Every day I aim to express some kind of praise — for something she has done that I appreciate, for the way she looks, or best of all, for who she is.

We often withhold expressions of admiration and thankfulness from those closest to us. The story is told of a taciturn gentleman in Vermont who eventually said to his wife, "When I think of how much you have meant to me all these years, it is almost more than I can do sometimes to keep from telling you so." The principle here is this: if you like it, say so. Charlie Shedd speaks of the matter of compliments concerning preparing a meal. He says:

> Do you realize, my dear boy, what a tremendous under taking it is to serve a good meal? Planning, buying, preparing, cooking, setting the table, dishing up, and then the whole messy business in reverse when it's over. In fact, one good meal is such an accomplishment that for you to sit there, devour it, and then hurry on back to your TV game without ever saying a good word must be a mortal sin. Of course I'm not God and I don't know the answer to the old argument about whether there are major and minor evils. But I've had to get up a few meals from beginning to end, and if there is a difference then neglecting to compliment the wife on a good dinner must be a very major error.
>
> There are some instances in which you would be a fool to pass up a 100% return on your investment. This is one of them and just seven words will do: "That was a great meal. Thank you!"[1]

When a husband begins to compliment his wife, there is a side benefit other than letting her know you appreciate her. Many wives have told me that, as their husbands compliment them, the children have begun to pick up the habit. They hear Dad compliment Mom, and so little four-year-old Junior begins to do the same thing. So when Mom comes home from the beauty parlor, he says, "Mom, you look great."

Then after dinner, "Mom, that was a terrific meal." That makes

Mom's day. But it is Dad who must set the pace.

So every day . . .

- *Speak* your love—tell her that you love her.
- *Demonstrate* your love by doing something nice for her.
- *Express* your love by paying her a sincere compliment.

The dividends are outstanding.

Note

1. Charlie Shedd, *Letters to Philip* (Garden City, N.Y.: Doubleday and Company, Inc., 1968), p. 24.

CHAPTER TWENTY-THREE

CHOOSING TO MAKE HER HAPPY

by Jack

I couldn't believe what I'd just heard. The group of young adults in our car had been laughing uproariously over some story that had been told when one of the women said wistfully, "I can never remember a time in my growing up years when my family ever laughed together."

My heart ached for her and for the parents she remembered who were without happiness. In my own life, I have been growing aware of the importance of the "habit of happiness" for people who are married. We have to cultivate it in ourselves and seek for it in our marriage partner.

I have often asked myself, "Do I have the 'habit of happiness'?" Do I make life exciting around our home? Do my wife and daughter think that it is enjoyable to live in this house with me?

As a husband and leader in our home, it struck me anew that this is my responsibility. Now most of us are not comedians. We may not have the capacity to be the life of a continual party in our leisure hours. But there is not one of us who couldn't use his imagination and his creativity to think about things that would produce a habit of happiness in his home — something God can and will help us do.

Instead of happiness, many men have honed to a fine point the "habit of gloom." When Dad walks in the door at the end of a tough day, watch out! He is liable to kick the dog first, then verbally kick everyone else in sight after that.

One friend of ours realized that despondency was something that was becoming his lifestyle. He determined to do something about it, and so he mentally started hanging all of his gloom and troubles on a certain telephone pole on his way home from work. The next morning when he went to the office, he'd pull them off the pole and take them to work with him. He told me that it has made a tremendous difference in the evenings around his home.

Christians have something much better to do with burdens than hang them on telephone poles, however. They can give them to Jesus Christ. Peter urged believers to cast "all your anxiety upon Him, because He cares for you" (1 Peter 5:7).

The problem isn't that our wives don't want to hear about the burdens with which we wrestle. They are usually quite interested in knowing about them. But it is our attitude toward these problems that makes the difference. Do we take out our frustrations on our wives and families, looking defeated and angry, or do we first commit them to the Lord and share with our wives from a vantage point of His peace?

When William Glasser, counselor and author of *Reality Therapy*, was lecturing in Colorado Springs, he stated he would not recommend marrying anyone who had never learned to laugh.

We need to develop a sense of humor that will enable us, at times, to be able to throw back our heads and howl with laughter. Life does have its humorous moments and we must learn to laugh, and to laugh at ourselves also. We all really blunder at times. If we cannot laugh at ourselves, it may indicate that we are taking ourselves too seriously. And taking ourselves too seriously can strain any relationship.

I read an article about resorts in Pennsylvania that cater to honeymooners. Besides the heart-shaped bathtubs and round beds, most of these resorts have full-time recreational directors. The astounding thing to me was that, according to the story, most of the couples take advantage of a packed schedule that goes on till the wee hours of the morning. The article speculated that the reason for this was that the honeymooners did not know each other well enough yet to know what to say when they were alone, so they kept themselves frantically busy with activity.

It is sad that this could be true with honeymooners. It is tragic that it is true with many couples married several years.

Do you and your mate enjoy each other when you aren't doing anything special? Do you relish your times of just talking after the kids have gone to bed? Or is this something you seldom do because you have long since run out of things to say unless it is a sentence during a TV commercial?

When a person is not growing in a relationship with God (see chapter 17), developing as an individual, stretching to become all that God meant him or her to be, then it isn't the other person who is boring. That person is really bored with himself or herself.

Developing an easy, enjoyable, growing relationship takes work. It doesn't just happen overnight. Part of that work involves asking God for ideas to develop the habit of happiness. Another is the determination to take time to develop a friendship with each other that is permeated with joy and pleasure in the other's company. This is worth any price it exacts.

Do you know what makes your wife happy? Are you concerned with her happiness? Most of the time it is the little things that count the most. When I asked Carole to name some of the little things she remembered that showed her I really cared, she mentioned that at least once a week when our daughter had colic as a baby, I would sleep on the davenport by her crib to try to help the pain and give Carole a good night's rest. (Wives frequently mention their husband's willingness to baby-sit so they can go shopping as one of the things they most appreciate about them.)

Carole also mentioned how much she felt loved when, on one

birthday when I had to be out of town, she got up to find in a dozen places around the house little "Happy Birthday" messages written with erasable pencil on the TV screen, on the back of the medicine cabinet door, on the mirror in our bathroom, and in many other visible places.

Women have an endless capacity for tenderness, devotion, and love. I have never heard one woman complain about her husband being too considerate. I am wondering if there is any woman anywhere who ever got too much affection.

Most men give a great deal of thought and consideration to details when it comes to their work. If they have a job that is the least bit creative, they are constantly trying to be innovative, to do their jobs better, to come up with new ideas. At work they are creative thinkers. But little of that creativity spills over in improving the love relationship with the person with whom they hope to spend all the years of their lives.

It is vital for a wife to know she is number one in her husband's thinking. For this we need time and careful thought.

Ask yourself this question: By my actions, how would my wife list these items in order of priority in my life? (Not what I say, or how I would list them, but by my *actions* how would my wife see my priorities?) They are alphabetical here:

- My children or family
- My favorite hobby or sport
- My job or career
- Ministry activities in which I am involved
- My relationship to God
- My wife

After listing these six items in priority order from your vantage point, ask your wife to list these as she sees them prioritized in your life. You may be in for a shock.

A wife needs to be convinced that, next to God, she is num-

ber one in your thoughts. She can figure out that there is a difference between being number one in thoughts and number one in
time. She obviously cannot be number one in the amount of time
you spend with her because you have to spend more hours on
your job than you are able to spend with her. In many little ways,
however, you communicate to her that she is, or is not, topmost
in your thinking.

Carole got a frantic phone call one night at ten o'clock. It was
from a wife who was trying to keep from pushing the panic but-
ton. Her husband had not returned home from work yet, and had
given her no indication that he was going to be late. She wanted
Carole to pray first, then help her decide if she should call the
police. Just as her torrent of words poured out, her husband non-
chalantly walked in the door. He had effectively communicated to
his wife that she was far from being a priority in his thoughts. To
her, this incident, multiplied many times, communicated that her
husband simply didn't care.

The neglect of little things, such as letting our wives know
when to expect us for dinner, keeping them knowledgeable of our
whereabouts, expressing interest in the details of their day, putting
their concerns ahead of our own, tell our wives, "You are a low
person on my priority list. I don't care about you that much." On
the other hand, consistently doing those things which mean so
much to her loudly declare, "You are important to me! You are
number one! I love you!"

It is essential to demonstrate our love for our wives. To do so
is to obey one of God's commandments. May God give us grace to
extend our love by words and actions daily, and to prove to our
mates that our love has no limits to its expression.

CHAPTER TWENTY-FOUR

CHOOSING TO ACCEPT

by Carole

Jack turned off the light and I lay quietly in the dark, my eyes adjusting to the soft blackness. He was leaving for Colorado the next morning to investigate a change of ministry for us. I knew he was excited, but a bit apprehensive.

I loved our present work in a large city church and had no desire to change. The thought of moving made me tired. Yet a few weeks before, God had nudged me in a very definite way. As I was reading in Deuteronomy (of all places), one verse seemed to glare at me as if lighted in neon. Moses had said, "See, the LORD your God has placed the land before you; go up, take possession, as the LORD, the God of your fathers, has spoken to you. Do not fear or be dismayed" (1:21).

I said to myself, "Carole, don't take this verse out of context. God said that to the nation of Israel."

But the still small Voice refused to be either still or small. My eyes kept being pulled to that one verse as God seemed to say to me, "Carole, take special note of this and be prepared."

I argued back, "I don't want to even think You might want us to move, Lord."

He responded in my heart, "I said, be ready."

So that evening, several weeks after my talk with the Lord about moving, just as we were about to fall asleep, I quite casually said to Jack, "Honey, if God leads you to take this job, please don't feel you have to wait and ask me about it. I am 100 percent with you in whatever God leads you to do."

There was a moment of silence. Then Jack gathered me in his arms and with a break in his voice said, "You can't know what that means to me!"

From his emotional response, I could tell it meant a great deal. Jack seldom has to choke back tears. And I was reminded for the one hundred and first time how vital it is to a man to know his wife is 100 percent behind him.

As a wife, I have two great fears in my life. One is that I would miss out on some wonderful thing that God has for me because of not being open to it. In the book of Lamentations God says that His mercies are new every morning and His faithfulness is great (3:23). I surely don't want to miss out on any of the riches that God has for me because I am too lazy or self-centered to search for them.

My second fear is that in some way I might hinder Jack in whatever God has for him to do, defeating him in God's work for his life. While this may be a "healthy fear," it is a scary one. I have watched wives defeat their husbands and in the process destroy them. Solomon said, "An excellent wife is the crown of her husband, but she who shames him is as rottenness in his bones" (Proverbs 12:4). In *The Living Bible*, that last part reads, "[She] corrodes his strength and tears down everything he does."

Dr. David Hubbard, former president of Fuller Theological Seminary, has said, "Marriage does not demand perfection, but it must be given priority. It is an institution for sinners. No one else need apply. But it finds its fullest glory when sinners see it as God's way of leading us to His ultimate curriculum of love and righteousness."[1]

Marriage is "God's way of leading us to His ultimate curriculum." I like that! And there are separate courses for husbands and for wives.

The wife's course is laid out by the Apostle Peter. I like the way the Amplified Bible renders it, for it takes the original Greek word and gives it all of its English meanings. Peter talks about wives having reverent and chaste behaviour, and the word reverent in its fuller meaning is described this way: "reverence includes—to respect, defer to, revere him; [revere means] to honor, esteem (appreciate, prize), and [in the human sense] adore him; [and adore means] to admire, praise, be devoted to, deeply love and enjoy [your husband]" (1 Peter 3:2, AMP).

That's all we need to do!

When I first read this list, I threw up my hands in frustration and thought, *No way!* And it is an impossible task . . . except for God. His grace, His power, His enabling is the only way we can ever come close to loving our husbands this way. I am excited about the fact that God never gives us a command that He won't enable us to carry out if we really turn it over to Him. He has commanded that we love our husbands—revere, honor, adore—and He will give us the grace to do it. Some may be thinking, *You don't know my husband!* And that's right, I don't. But God knows him and that promise is not limited by any husband's character.

Love is an expression of our wills, not just our feelings. Sometimes only our wills are involved. Many times the feelings will follow an act of our wills to love. A wife may ask, "But isn't it being a hypocrite to tell him I love him when I don't feel any love for him?"

The answer is no. We may need to will to love first—to act and talk in a loving way—to demonstrate love because we want to obey God.

A woman wrote the following letter to Dr. Clyde Narramore, well-known Christian counselor:

One day I was saved and I began to know what God could do for me. Was love something that you felt, something that happened to you, or an act of the will? I finally faced the fact that I might not be able to feel love, but why could I not show forth love? From that moment on I began to behave as if I did feel love! What would I do for my husband today, I asked myself, if I really were in love with him? Then I proceeded to do these little kindnesses. I studied his likes and dislikes, and bought little treats for his lunch box. I tried to comfort him when he came home from work tired or harassed by a heavy schedule. I met him at the door with a smile. I respected his discipline of the children and worked with him. I tried to speak softly and diplomatically when we had differences. I listened to him.

Soon, I noticed a marked change in him. He was behaving as though he were living with someone who loved him! And I began to notice a change in my own feelings. He was not at all like I had concluded. He had real depth. And I was beginning to fall in love with him!

Is this why God admonishes us all to show forth love? He has not said to show forth love if you feel love, has He? At the time, it seemed to me that Christians did all the giving and none of the getting. But, when God told my heart to show forth love, it was really I who was blessed in the end.[2]

The Holy Spirit will give us a spirit of love flowing through us. He will give strength to demonstrate love as well as the feeling of love. I won't minimize the need for the feeling; it is tremendously important to me. But some wives may need to will to love first and let the feelings come in God's time.

True acceptance is perhaps one of the most difficult ways of expressing our love. And one of the most vital.

The first time I heard Jack say that he was the president of the Carole Mayhall Fan Club was at a conference in Colorado where he spoke to the husbands with the wives present. He went on and on about my being a good cook (he thinks I am, but his favorite meal is a pot roast, put in the oven with a can of mushroom soup on it, and cooked to death), a good mother, a good just-about-everything, which isn't even fractionally true.

As he was saying all those lovely things, you can imagine how it affected me. I was deeply touched. In our room after the meeting, I went to him, put my arms around him, and said, "Thank you for saying such wonderful things about me tonight. But how come you didn't tell them some of the bad things as well?"

He responded, "Because I don't remember any!"

That is acceptance!

Literally speaking, his statements were not true. Jack knows me well. He knows my faults and is aware of some ugly things in my life.

But he accepts me. And I want to accept him in that complete kind of way. It is God's job to make our husbands good. It is our job to make them happy. And one of the ways we can make them most happy is by accepting them.

John Powell tells of talking to a friend while he was writing his book *Why Am I Afraid to Tell You Who I Am?* The friend said, "Do you want an answer to your question?"

The author replied, "Well, that's the purpose of the book, to answer the question."

So his friend said, "But do you want my answer?"

John Powell said he did.

So his friend said, "I am afraid to tell you who I am, because, if I tell you who I am, you may not like who I am, and it's all that I have."[3]

Most people will not be open with us unless they feel accepted. They can risk vulnerability only if they know they are accepted with all their faults, hang-ups, and idiosyncrasies. Acceptance is felt.

We might ask, How many "why" questions do you use each day with the person to whom you are married? Have you ever considered that a "why" question is threatening and that it may be an indication of how much or how little you are truly accepting?

I am not talking about information type "why" questions, but questions such as, Why did you turn there? Why are you late? Why did you forget your raincoat? Why wouldn't you let me go? Why did you do it that way? These are all the type of questions which shout, "I wouldn't have turned there, been late, forgotten my raincoat, done it that way." You may not mean the question to suggest that (though it just could be that you did), but that is the way such questions often come across.

One winter our cable TV went out on the set in our bedroom. After calling the repairman for two weeks with no results, Jack ingeniously ran a long wire down the hall and hooked up another cable so we could have a picture on our bedroom set.

One Saturday afternoon the repairman showed up, and as I answered the door, he abruptly asked, "Do you have a picture?"

Well, we did have a picture, but only thanks to my husband's genius and an ugly wire running the entire length of the hallway. I answered the repairman's question before I explained the whole situation by saying, "Yes . . ."

Jack heard this from the upstairs hallway and, realizing what the repairman meant, interrupted our conversation. "No," he said, "we don't have a picture." He then proceeded to show the man what had happened.

As he was following the man outside, going back and forth, Jack walked through the kitchen and said, "Why did you tell him we had a picture?" Without pausing long enough for me to say anything, he went outside.

As the saying goes, I stood there with egg on my face! I felt immediately and giantly . . . stupid. And hurt.

My head was saying logically, "Carole, Jack did not mean to hurt you," but my heart was saying, "Ouch." A great, big chunk of ice lay between what my head was saying and what my heart was feeling.

His "why" question had done it.

Now (just so you'll have the ending to this incident), I am

learning not to harbor hurt feelings. So as Jack was rushing through again, I stopped him. "I am feeling very stupid as a result of what you said," I managed to get out.

"What did I say?" he inquired with great concern. (I knew he hadn't meant it deliberately.)

When I told him, he quickly apologized. "Honey, I didn't mean to hurt you. I'm sorry. Will you forgive me?"

That big block of ice melted—there wasn't even a puddle left.

A good checkup on your AQ (Acceptance Quotient) is to see if you can go a whole week without asking an intimidating "why" question . . . then a whole month . . . and then strike it from your vocabulary altogether. The elimination of threatening questions can be a practical means of helping your loved ones feel your acceptance. And in acceptance, freedom. And in freedom, love.

Notes
1. Dr. David Hubbard, used by permission.
2. From *A Woman's World* by Dr. Clyde M. Narramore, p. 148. Copyright © 1963 by Zondervan Publishing House, Grand Rapids, Mich. Used by permission.
3. John Powell, *Why Am I Afraid to Tell You Who I Am?* (Niles, Ill.: Argus Communications, 1969), p. 12.

CHAPTER TWENTY-FIVE

CHOOSING
TO APPRECIATE
AND ADMIRE

by Carole

Cisco, Utah. Mentally my mind said it, Ceezco, the way the Cisco Kid's sidekick used to pronounce it in the western movies many long years ago.

And "Ceezco" looked just like it sounded. Bypassed by the Interstate many years before, all that remained of the town were four weather-beaten shells of former motels, the skeletons of two filling stations, hulks of old houses, and Ethel's Cafe.

We pulled up in front of Ethel's to meet our fellow rafters to begin a two-day white-water trip through the canyons of Utah.

I thought about Cisco and our exciting day as I lay staring into the black sky that night. I pulled my sleeping bag (more appropriately termed my "lying awake" bag) over my side and wiggled to find a more comfortable position on my tiny back-pad.

This was a trip I'd wanted to take for years, and God had finally arranged it . . . with our daughter, her husband, and several other special friends. We were on an adventure trip that proved to be, as Lynn later put it, "One which met all our expectations and none of our fears." It was great.

I looked over at Jack, sleeping beside me, and a great wave of feeling engulfed me. I wanted to wake him up, throw my arms around him, and say, "Hey, I appreciate you." It had been my enthusiasm which had fanned the trip-flame, but it took Jack's love and consideration to make it possible. I took a few minutes to thank the Lord for a husband who gives of himself.

What exactly is appreciation?

A few years ago we moved to Colorado after being in the Chicago area for fourteen years. We had formed some deep friendships in those fourteen years, and I found after moving that I was lonely. I went through a period of six months of rather difficult adjustment to our new situation.

This adjustment caused me to realize that my mother had moved about the same time of her life. Shortly after his three children had left home to be married or to go to college, Daddy had changed jobs. Mother went from a town where she was well-known in the community, away from a church in which she was active and knew everyone, left a large old rambling home she loved, and moved into a little crackerbox-house in another state where she knew no one. Yet I never heard her complain.

When I went to visit my mother after our move, I asked her about her move. I described our similar state of affairs in moving, my loneliness, and then said, "Mom, I never heard one word of complaint or grumbling from you. How come?"

Mother's eyes widened in surprise, and she looked shocked by my question. She said, "Why Carole, I was with your father!" That is appreciation.

Mrs. Norman Vincent Peale has said:

Every person needs to feel that he marches at the head of some other person's parade, that his happiness and welfare come first, ahead of all happiness and welfares. This sense of being able to claim complete priority in another person's affections is the cornerstone of marriage, but the only way a person can be sure he has this priority is when the other person sends clear, frequent, unambiguous signals confirming it. It is not enough to love someone routinely or passively or mutely.[1]

Jack and I were sitting in a coffee shop one afternoon, discussing the question of priorities. He asked me how I knew I was number one after God on his priority list. I recalled several incidents that more than proved to me my status in his life, such as the time he canceled a business trip to take care of me when I had caught the mumps from our daughter Lynn and was very ill. I looked like a horror at the time, but he didn't even comment on my grotesque appearance, which added saintliness to his virtues.

When I asked his question back to him, he said, "I know that I am on the top of your priority list because you tell me. I may not be greatly responsive when you compliment me [sometimes he acts embarrassed, or responds in a more subdued way than I would], but I really appreciate all the nice things you say."

Solomon stated, "A man hath joy by the answer of his mouth; and a word spoken in due season, how good is it!" (Proverbs 15:23, KJV).

Joy comes into our lives and marriages as we learn to speak many "good words" to those we love, but especially to that one God has chosen to be our partner for life.

Besides learning to appreciate, we must grow in the ability to *admire*.

⊛

"I really don't like this restaurant," my friend murmured under her breath. "But it's one of Bill's favorites." It was quickly obvious that it was not one of hers.

As we dined that evening, I thought the old world atmosphere delightful, the food good, and the service excellent. But from the barrage of disparaging comments, it became blatantly apparent that we were here only because Bill had chosen it over his wife's disapproval. She had made up her mind not to like that restaurant, and not even Maxim's of Paris would have pleased her that summer evening.

The signals she telegraphed were clearly sent and pointedly received. She did not approve of her husband. Yes, I said of her husband. She may have thought she was criticizing a restaurant, but her verbal stabs at the food, the noise, and the service were aimed with accuracy at his taste, his choice, his manners. And she was drawing blood.

Inwardly I thought, *Oh, please, don't.* In our women's group, we had been studying ways to encourage our husbands, and one of the most effective ways to encourage is by expressing admiration . . . to encourage and build instead of "corroding his strength and tearing down everything he does" (Proverbs 12:4, TLB). One of the greatest ministries a wife can have in her husband's life is the ministry of encouragement through admiration. Not flattery, but sincere praise. My friend was striving to build—but she had just torn away several months of effort . . . and probably wasn't even aware of what she had done.

The most objective man I know becomes totally subjective when his wife belittles him or expresses disapproval of something he has chosen, be it a restaurant or a gift.

I can almost hear someone saying, "But what if I don't like what he has given me or the restaurant he has chosen? Isn't it wrong to be dishonest and say that I like it when I don't?"

Another friend of mine learned a valuable lesson in this area. Her husband was not yet a Christian, and she had been trying to show Christ's love to him. They had had some major problems in the years before she invited Christ to take over her life. Then, for her birthday, he had given her some bathroom towels. She didn't think that was a very personal gift and was disappointed; she hated the color of the towels (she is a warm orange-yellow-red person, and the color he chose was beige), and when she asked him if she minded if she exchanged them for another color, he had said, "Yes, I do mind." Period.

Now how was she in all honesty supposed to be grateful for those towels?

God taught her something through that incident. As she prayed about it, God reminded her of the years her husband hadn't given her any remembrance on her birthday. This year, he had made the effort to shop, buy, and wrap a present for her. She was appreciative of that. So while she couldn't honestly rave over beige towels, she could and did express warm gratitude for the love and time of her husband (and she bought bright colored washcloths to go with the towels).

That is one wise woman.

Perhaps the old saying "If you can't think of something nice to say, don't say anything" is a good one to follow in situations like this. If you have gone out to eat at a real "bummer," and nothing is right except the water and even that is served in a dirty glass, the important thing is for the other person to know that you are glad to be with him. All else can be ignored. Your husband is not dumb enough to take you there again, anyhow.

Many questions puzzle our minds when it comes to expressing admiration to our husbands. Here are some of the most common.

One question that is asked often is: Won't it make my husband proud if I keep complimenting and admiring him?

The answer is no. The Bible says, "Do not withhold good from those to whom it is due, when it is in your power to do it" (Proverbs 3:27). Sincere praise costs little. If it is "in the power of your hand to do it" (AMP), then God says not to withhold it. So you are disobeying God when you fail to compliment and encourage your husband (and others as well). I can never thank the Lord enough for a mother and father who constantly affirmed me. I didn't believe them when they told this gangling girl with braces on her teeth that she was beautiful, but it certainly built security and a feeling of being loved into my life. And I guess to them, I *was* beautiful. Their esteem didn't make me proud—except of my great parents.

We all long for admiration. Women tend to compliment other women and receive admiration from their small children. But men seldom praise each other. Perhaps this is why they have a greater need along this line. But a man hungers for admiration, and it is vital to him. And if you are not the source of the encouragement he needs, someone else may be.

Another frequent and searching question is: I'm always complimenting my husband, but he continues to cut me down. I don't have any resources left—I can't go on. What do I do?

No easy answer exists for this one.

A wife once asked me, "What do you do when you have knocked yourself out preparing a good meal for your husband and he says, 'That was the lousiest meal I've ever eaten'?"

I almost responded with, "Cry a lot," but that wouldn't have helped her.

She went on to explain that she really tried to show her husband how much she loved him and tried to compliment him, but he kept cutting her down. She was just too tired to keep on trying.

As we talked, she admitted that her husband had a low self-image and didn't like himself or think he was any good. So I asked her if, when she complimented him, she thought he really heard her. After considering this question, she answered, "No, he probably doesn't hear me."

Many people have such a low estimation of themselves that they simply sluff off any compliment given them. But they pick up in flashing neon lights any slight, slur, complaint, or negative tone of voice. Then, in order to try to build themselves up, they put others down, especially their spouse. The cycle spirals ever downward.

Someone has to break into that vicious cycle, and it can be the Christian spouse. The first thing a wife may have to do is to ask a creative God for ideas on how to express admiration for her husband in a way that he will hear. To pray that God will open inroads to his heart and give him a God-confidence, so that he will have a greater self-confidence. It will take time and patience. But our God is a miracle-working God.

As we continued talking, I suggested to this woman that she pray for ideas on how to get through to her husband, whom she sincerely loved and admired . . . new ways that she hadn't tried before. Ways such as never failing to tell him a "third person compliment." Wives should never miss the opportunity of telling their husbands nice things someone else has said about them.

Another way is to start with compliments he might really believe. If a wife told her overweight husband that she admired his physique, he may think she was putting him on even if she were sincere; but if she told him how much she appreciated the way he worked so hard to provide for her and the children, he might believe her. She could also express admiration in non-verbal ways. At the heart and core of this is the physical expression of love. A wife can defeat every nice remark she has made all day if she is not wholehearted in making her husband feel like a man in bed at night. (More on this in a later chapter.) But many wives have given up on even the little expressions of love such as greeting him at the door with a kiss and a smile, being dressed up just for him, planning special dinners — things you have heard about all your life but are inclined to let slide after several years of marriage.

Have you convinced your husband that his coming home is the high point of your day?

In her book *One Plus One Equals One*, Kay Arvin describes the negative of that situation:

Charles said it well, simply and clearly. "You know, when I get home after work, the only one who acts as if she cares at all is my little dog. She really is glad to see me and lets me know it. Maybe everybody is, I don't know. But you can't tell it. I always come in the back door because Doris is in the kitchen about then, usually. But she always looks up from whatever she is doing with the most startled look, and says, 'Oh, are you home already?' She says it like she really means, 'Surely you're not home already!' Somehow she makes me feel like I've done the wrong thing, just by getting home. I used to try and say hello to the kids, but I don't do that anymore. Seems I would get in between them and the TV set at just the wrong minute, and the darn thing was on so loud they couldn't hear what I said anyway—when they were home, that is, which they usually weren't. So now, I just pick up little Suzy, my dog, stick her under my arm and go out in the yard. I act like I don't care, and maybe I shouldn't really—but I do. It gives me the feeling that all I am hanging around there for is just to pay the bills and keep the place up. You know, I believe that if the bills were taken care of and nothing broke, I bet I could be gone a whole week and nobody would even notice it."

Charles felt like stomping his feet and yelling, "Hey, please somebody, look happy just a little that I've come home again. Don't shut me out. Doggone it, I'm glad to be here; somebody be glad with me." But he was an uncomplicated, well-mannered man, and instead of stomping and yelling, he quietly swallowed his hurt, took the little dog under his arm, and went out into the backyard to play with her. The hurt pride didn't disappear though but followed the course of many small hurts which, through repetition, grew into resentment.[2]

Our marriages rest on such things!

It became apparent as I talked to the wife whose husband had criticized her meal so cruelly that her idea of being a godly wife was never to express a negative feeling. It was no wonder she was coming apart at the seams. Her anger had as many quills as a porcupine and she was unconsciously sending them to stick in her husband's flesh. No, she hadn't told him how his cutting remarks were hurting her. She wasn't even letting her husband know her—not the real inside vulnerable part of her, anyway.

In love, she needed to tell her husband how she felt when he made a remark like, "That was the lousiest meal I ever ate." It hurt her. It made her feel like giving up and never cooking meals again. It tore her apart and made her want to chew nails. So she should tell him . . . but in love.

Now God is concerned with how we express ourselves. He says, "It is better to dwell in a corner of the housetop [on the flat oriental roof, exposed to all kinds of weather] than in a house shared with a nagging, quarrelsome and faultfinding woman" (Proverbs 21:9, AMP). And very descriptively Solomon said, "As a ring of gold in a swine's snout, so is a beautiful woman who lacks discretion" (11:22). Discretion to me means knowing when to speak and when to keep quiet. I wish I had more discretion!

How can we express a negative in a positive way? Many books have been written about how to do it, but one of the most help-ful truths that I have picked up from them is expressing our feel-ings in "I" statements, "I am feeling hurt and angry," rather than the accusatory "you" statements, "You make me mad when you do that." In order to be faithful to our husbands and to ourselves, we must be honest, but we need love and wisdom to be honest in the right way. "Never forget to be truthful and kind. Hold these virtues tightly. Write them deep within your heart" (Proverbs 3:3, TLB). And always there should be the positive, "Anxiety in the heart of a man weights it down, but a good word makes it glad" (12:25). If we surround our husbands with praise and admiration, and if we build up an atmosphere and climate of love and appreciation, a small squall on the horizon isn't going to do anything but clear the air. But if the weather isn't usually sunny, then a cloudburst can wash away many good words.

So, if your husband has a habit of cutting you down contin-ually, remember these four things:

1. Ask God for ideas to get through to him that you sincerely love and admire him.
2. Pray that God would change his heart and give him a more positive self-image so that he can respond lovingly to you.
3. Be honest in your feelings and "speak the truth in love."
4. Ask God for the strength to keep on loving and admiring him till you break into and reverse that downward cycle of ego-destruction.

Another question frequently heard is: How do I admire and encourage my husband in practical ways?

Some suggested answers are:

1. Pray every day for the ability to be an encourager. Ask God for opportunities to say that "good word"—not just to your husband, but to everyone you meet. God can use this ability to make you a breath of blessing to those around you and the dividends are way out of proportion to the time invested.
2. Keep a list of how other women show admiration for their husbands. Paul said that the older women are to teach the younger women to "love their husbands" (Titus 2:4). Now I don't know how anyone can teach another to feel love, so I take this to mean that the older women (both spiritually and in age) should teach the younger women to demonstrate love for their husbands. Make a point to ask older women how they express love. Ask your husband in what ways you are an encouragement to him, and then ask him for his suggestions as to how you might be more of an encouragement to him.
3. Compliment him every day. Some books will tell you that a man prefers to be complimented for his "manly"

characteristics, such as his physical strength and ability to lead. But I really doubt that there is anything that a man would resent in the way of a sincere compliment. Remember, too, to repeat compliments from others.

4. Be a grateful wife—accept his gifts with love and pleasure.

5. And remember, if you don't admire your husband, then ask God for a truly loving, admiring heart and start acting like you think he is wonderful. Feelings often follow actions. If we waited for the feelings, many of us would never act.

Our husbands need to know, feel, and be the number one person in our lives. God grant that it be so.

Notes

1. Mrs. Norman Vincent Peale, used by permission.
2. Kay K. Arvin, *One Plus One Equals One*, pp. 37-38. © Copyright 1969 Broadman Press, Nashville, Tenn. All rights reserved. Used by permission.

CHAPTER TWENTY-SIX

CHOOSING TO GROW

by Jack

I came in the front door whistling, pausing to hang my jacket in the hall closet. Usually, Carole would come from some part of the house to greet me when I arrived home from work, but this night all I heard were small sounds coming from the kitchen. The year was 1956.

"Hi, honey," I called through the length of the house.

"Hello," came the response from the recesses of the kitchen.

The chill in her tone signaled that something was wrong. *What have I done now?* I wondered.

Optimistically, I thought I might be able to avoid a quarrel, so I walked into the kitchen, gave Carole a quick hug, and forcing cheerfulness, asked, "Have a good day?"

"Yes," came her monotoned response. (Translation: "I haven't, and it's all your fault!")

"Anything wrong?" I queried.

"No," she answered. (Translation: "You have to ask me some more before I'll tell you.")

We had been married a few years and these clashes had formed a pattern. I would do something that Carole didn't like, and she would withdraw in cold silence till I finally asked enough times to find out what the problem was. Then, none too gently, she would tell me.

Since I had a temper also, I would snap back and defend myself, or be silently hostile. Fortunately, Carole gets over her anger quickly once she has told me her feelings, and she would apologize, or I would, and things would be peaceful again.

Our problem was that the conflicts were becoming more frequent and violent and we could not fathom either the cause or find the solution. The result was a great deal of frustration in both of us.

But that evening, though neither of us can remember what the initial dispute was about, we remember that God took charge in a way we hadn't anticipated.

"I know there is something bothering you. Tell me what it is," I persisted.

She told me then, in detail, and in anger.

I was ready to lash back. But instead, God spoke through a verse I had learned that week. "Jack, you have need of patience, that, after you have done the will of God, you might receive the promise" (see Hebrews 10:36, KJV).

At once, I felt a love and tenderness toward Carole that was not at all like me in these kinds of heated situations, and I heard myself saying, "Well, you are right. I'm sorry. Why don't we pray about it together?"

Carole, shocked, was silent. And I did pray. The next moment her arms were around me and she was saying, "I'm sorry too, honey. Please forgive me."

In a graphic way that evening, both of us saw how learning Scripture is life-changing and habit-changing.

I hadn't been memorizing Scripture for long. A few weeks prior to this incident, I'd had lunch with Skip Gray, Navigator representative in the area, and in the course of talking about some things I'd heard at a conference, he pulled out a little packet of cards with Bible verses printed on them. Over the lunch hour, he offered to give me the packet if I would memorize the four verses it contained. So I rose to the challenge, took the packet, and memorized the four verses. When I knew the four verses word-perfect, I met Skip again the following week, and he checked me out on them.

Then he said, "Why don't you start using the *Topical Memory System* of The Navigators? It will help you learn how to memorize Scripture."[1]

I followed his advice and at the time of our quarrel I had memorized a number of verses, which were planted firmly in my heart. When Carole told me what I had done that morning to hurt her, the Spirit of God took one of those verses and applied it to my life. How grateful I am that He did.

This was our first real encounter with what God's Word could do in a real, live situation on a moment's notice. And it was the beginning of a brand new dimension in our marriage relationship. Carole realized the difference God's Word was beginning to make in my life and it wasn't long before she began to memorize some verses also. As both of us applied these scriptures to our lives, God began to change us in practical, shoe-leather ways.

For the time invested, there is no other way of getting the Word of God into our lives that has more meaning, is more life-changing, and has more significance than memorizing verses and passages from the Bible — putting them in our hearts for the Spirit of God to use. This is still a continual source of help to me as I have made it a habit of life.

Polls have shown that the average Christian, regardless of how long he or she has been a Christian, has memorized, with references, twelve verses of Scripture. How tragic that is. The resources of God can be just a thought away, but instead lie buried in His Book. If you were to memorize only one verse a week and review these verses regularly, in one year your life would be enriched by fifty-two verses that God could use anywhere, anytime. That is over four times what most Christians know. And there is not one of you who couldn't do it.

Scripture verses do have to be reviewed once we have learned them. Our minds are similar to a grassy yard in a corner lot. If the lot is on the way to the local school and the kids start taking a short-cut across it in order to get to school three seconds sooner, the first few days their steps will not be noticed. But in a couple of weeks, a path will become visible and in a month only bare dirt will remain.

When we put something through our minds enough times, it is going to wear a pathway in our brain that will remain. We remember our phone numbers and our addresses because of constant repetition. So it is with memorizing Scripture.

God has said through the Apostle Paul:

I urge you therefore, brethren, by the mercies of God, to present your bodies a living and holy sacrifice, acceptable to God, which is your spiritual service of worship. And do not be conformed to this world, but be transformed by the renewing of your mind, that you may prove what the will of God is, that which is good and acceptable and perfect. (Romans 12:1-2)

Being conformed to this world is a process that takes place over a long period of time. Having our minds "renewed by God" is also a process that takes place by our allowing our minds to be influenced by the way God thinks—which is written down in the pages of His Word. The more we expose our thinking to His Word, the more our minds are remade from within and we begin to think on parallel lines with God. If we want God to change us "from one degree of glory to another" (2 Corinthians 3:18, AMP), if we want to be conformed to the image of His Son, if we want to become the kinds of husbands and wives who will grow in love and godliness, an excellent way to progress is by allowing God to invade our lives through His Word as we learn it by heart.

Note
1. The *Topical Memory System* and other Navigator memory materials are available from your local Christian bookstore.

PART FIVE

RESPONSIBILITIES

CHAPTER TWENTY-SEVEN

CHOOSING TO LEAD

by Jack

Confusion: kan-'fyu-zhan. 1: an act or instance of confusing;
2: the quality or state of being confused.[1]

Generally speaking, the husband's responsibility in the home today
is in a state of confusion.

Colonel Baron George Von Trapp whistles a series of signals
and his children tumble down the stairs, line up in descending
order by age, and stand at attention while an astonished Maria
looks on. Some men seem to look on this scene from "Sound of
Music" as the way to be the biblical heads of their homes. They are
confused about what constitutes biblical leadership.

Contractual marriage is being touted among certain groups in
our society today. The adherents claim that to sign a marriage con-
tract which spells out all responsibilities and decisions, splitting
them equally between the man and the woman will lead to freedom and harmony. They are confused about what constitutes a
biblical marriage.

Distorted views are making the rounds these days on the subject of leadership within Christian marriage. Many are arguing with
God's plan; some do not really understand it; others don't want to
believe it. They are confused.

What is God's plan for leadership in a marriage? What does the term headship mean?

I remember as a boy being fascinated by our county fair. I loved it all — the crowds, the grandstand show, the exhibits — but most of all I enjoyed the midway with its rides and sideshows. At one fair, the big attraction at one of the sideshows was a two-headed monster. Paying my dime (that's how long ago it was!), I went in and was at the same time horrified and fascinated to see a cow with a second head growing out of its neck at an angle. It was grotesque.

A two-headed anything is a mistake of nature and is considered a freak. And two heads in a marriage relationship is no different. God is not in the business of making monsters. He created the marriage union with one head only.

In my work, I've had the opportunity to make several detailed studies on leadership, and the information I obtained has helped me understand both the responsibilities of leadership and the principles involved in being a leader. The responsibilities are awesome and the principles are difficult. I'd just as soon abdicate at times, but to do so would be to disobey God. For His Word has clearly stated, "The husband is the head of the wife, as Christ also is the head of the church, He Himself being the Savior of the body. But as the church is subject to Christ, so also the wives ought to be to their husbands in everything" (Ephesians 5:23-24). Some people try desperately to run around this passage of Scripture. However, it must be faced head-on and reckoned with as part of God's overall plan for marriage.

The husband is to be the head, the leader of his wife. The Bible states that this is to be a leadership of love, and love and authority are intertwined in this passage. Leadership without love usually results in tyranny; but in marriage, love without leadership leads to unstable, fanciful romanticism. A right balance of responsible authority and unselfish love must be maintained. Difficult? Yes. Impossible really without the wisdom and strength of the Holy Spirit.

BASIC RESPONSIBILITIES

In my study of leadership, I discovered that the two basic responsibilities of any leader are to watch out for the welfare of his people
and to accomplish the mission or goals on which the people have
decided. God has given us a beautiful example of leadership in
the life of David. "He also chose David His servant, and took him
from the sheepfolds; from the care of the ewes with suckling lambs
He brought him, to shepherd Jacob His people, and Israel His
inheritance. So he [David] shepherded them according to the
integrity of his heart, and guided them with his skillful hands"
(Psalm 78:70-72). David cared for his people—he watched out
for their welfare—and he guided them to accomplish the goals
that God had given.

For a husband to be a godly leader of his home, both of these
responsibilities need to be kept in mind. It is his job to watch out
for his wife and children and to guide his family with skill in those
goals which they have purposed together to achieve.

What are your goals as a husband and wife? Have you ever
talked about them or written them down—both short-range and
long-range? What is it that you want to accomplish in the next
year, five years, ten years as the result of your lives and marriage?

One long-range goal worth considering is to exemplify Christ
in your home, to create such an environment and atmosphere in
your relationship together that your love will be a picture of Christ's
love for His Church, to manifest in your home the fruit of the Holy
Spirit: love, joy, peace, longsuffering, gentleness, goodness, meek-
ness, faith (Galatians 5:22-23). This is a lifetime goal worth working for. This goal will then need to be broken up into bite-sized
portions by shorter range goals, perhaps doing some topical Bible
studies on each of these characteristics with your family, discussing
with them ways of demonstrating love in everyday life.

The prophet Malachi suggests another goal to consider (see
Malachi 2:13-16). He talks about what is on the Lord's heart for us

and sums it up in two words: "godly offspring." I believe this means both physical children and spiritual children—those we have led to Christ or "adopted" as God has directed us. To produce godly offspring takes sacrifice, determination, and prayer. But is there a more worthy goal?

It has been said that there are two things from our present world that are going to last forever. These are the Word of God and people. "Heaven and earth will pass away, but My words shall not pass away," Jesus told us (Matthew 24:35). The Word of God will endure forever.

And people will last for eternity. "For God so loved the world, that He gave His only begotten Son, that whoever believes in Him should not perish, but have eternal life" (John 3:16). We should invest our lives in that which is eternal . . . which will bring eternal rewards. Paul exemplified the joy of doing this when he said to the Thessalonians: "For who is our hope or joy or crown of exultation? Is it not even you, in the presence of our Lord Jesus at His coming? For you are our glory and joy" (1 Thessalonians 2:19-20).

It is the responsibility of the husband to watch out for the welfare of his wife and children, and to ensure that he and his wife are accomplishing, as a couple, those goals for which God has put them together.

PRINCIPLES OF GOOD LEADERSHIP

In the vast amount of research done on the subject of leadership, it has been discovered that leaders who practiced certain principles were successful no matter what their fields might have been. But leaders who were not successful constantly violated these same principles.

That research says quite a bit to me. While these are not hard and fast rules, leadership principles are good guidelines and are certainly applicable to a husband who wants to be a loving leader of his family. We want to explore a few of these principles in this and the next chapters. I am trying with the help of God to practice them.

Principle number one—Know your wife in order to look out for her welfare. Most men simply do not know their wives. Take the following brief quiz by mentally answering these five questions:

- What is your wife's greatest concern right now?
- What is her greatest need?
- What is her wildest dream?
- What causes her a small amount of pain?
- What new vista would she like to explore?

Can you answer these questions with certainty? If not, you don't, at the moment, know your wife. And if you don't know her, it will be very difficult for you to look out for her welfare. Perhaps she needs physical rest or time away from the children. Or she has a spiritual need and needs to pray with you. She may need encouragement; she may need to be noticed because she has been feeling like a part of your landscape you are not seeing. She may need an understanding heart, a listening ear, a word of appreciation, a new dress, a diverting interest, to share in a recreational hobby or sport with you, or a vacation. You may be saying, "Whatever it is, I can't afford it." But if you want to be God's kind of husband, you can't afford not to know—in order to try to meet that need she may have in her life.

Principle number two—Keep the channels of communication open and clear. The lack of a deep level of communication is the recognized number one problem in most marriages. And clear communication is vital to the success and growth of a marriage. It is not only important in knowing one another, it is essential for the high morale of your entire family. If you want a happy wife, take the responsibility for communicating on a deep level with her, to let her know what is going on in your innermost person.

Paul tells us that husbands are to love their wives in the same way as Christ loved the Church (Ephesians 5:25), and to lead their wives in that way too. Now who took the initiative in communicating—Christ or the Church? Christ took the initiative to open doors of communication with His people. If husbands are to exemplify Christ, then it is their responsibility to take the initiative in communicating clearly.

Carole and I have the opportunity to present some of these principles in marriage seminars in many parts of the country from time to time. We hear a common complaint from wives as we talk about the matter of communication. They say that their husbands not only fail to initiate communication, but they are reluctant to cooperate even when their wives suggest it. Many of these husbands would be aghast if they were told that they were disobeying God in this lack of initiative and cooperation. We then suggest some practical assignments and questions[2] to these couples to stimulate their exploring each other's hearts.

So know your wife and communicate clearly with her. It is your responsibility. You can't know her unless you do communicate, so these two principles go hand in hand. Through God's help, you can grow and mature together.

Notes

1. By permission. From *Webster's New Collegiate Dictionary*. © 1977 by G. & C. Merriam Co., Publishers of the Merriam-Webster Dictionaries, p. 238.
2. The assignments we give are selected questions from the "Discussion Questions for Better Communication," found at the end of this book, beginning on page 247.

CHAPTER TWENTY-EIGHT

CHOOSING HEADSHIP

by Jack

"You won't believe this, folks," Lynn, our daughter, wrote from college, "but my room is the neatest on the whole floor."

She was right on two counts—it was the neatest room on the floor and we had an extremely difficult time believing it.

In Lynn's growing years, Carole and I had tried every means we could think of to get Lynn to keep her room orderly. But somehow her idea of a clean room and our idea of it weren't even on speaking terms.

She confided to us later in her first year of college, "I guess I was just so used to seeing things picked up that I couldn't stand a mess." And now she wins the blue ribbon for order in her own home.

To continue with our discussion of key principles from the previous chapter, the best method of teaching and of leading is to set an example, which brings us to:

Principle number three—Set an example. It is impossible for a husband to ask or expect his wife and family to do something that he doesn't consider important enough to do himself.

Are you an example to your family in having a consistent time with God each day? Do you memorize God's Word? Do you study it? Are you hospitable, courteous, and honest? Whatever virtue you may want to see in your children has got to begin with you.

The phone rings late on Friday evening. Junior answers it, and it's for Dad. Now Dad has had one of the worst weeks in years. He's absolutely exhausted and mad at the whole world. Without thinking, he says, "Tell him I'm not here." Honesty will never be established as a value in that home if Dad has no integrity. The responsibility and privilege of husbands is to set an example.

Principle number four—Make sound and timely decisions. Make them; don't abdicate them. To make good decisions takes much thought and work, but they are absolutely vital. A businessman told me that he can hire people to do everything but two things—think and do things in the order of their importance.

But God will help us think. One of the tremendous assets of being in touch with God through Jesus Christ is that He will help us in making our decisions. The Lord has promised us in His Word that He will instruct us and guide us in the way that we should go. He will guide us with His eye being on us (Psalm 32:8). Many times a decision boils down to determining together what the will of God is. What does He want us to do in this situation? The road may have only one fork in it, or there may be a dozen things involved in the decision. But God has a way for us to go.

Scripture contains many concrete instructions—the "thou shalts" and the "thou shalt nots." We can usually figure these out without too much trouble, but obeying them may be another matter.

Between the "thou shalts" and the "thou shalt nots," however, are many things life brings along on which decisions have to be made. It may be that no specific verse gives us direction or guidance on this decision, so we have to look for other means.

It is a beautiful thing that God has given us principles to operate on in these areas, and He has implanted the Holy Spirit in our hearts to speak to us and say, "This is what I want you to do." The still small voice of the Holy Spirit of God will often guide us.[1]

A number of years ago I was in California after the Christmas holidays attending a conference in the San Francisco Bay area. After the conference I went to visit my parents in the Los Angeles area before flying back to Chicago. At the same time, another staff couple from Michigan had driven out to the conference in a Volkswagen with their six-month-old baby, Deborah. That's a long, hard trip in a VW.

After the conference was over, the couple got an idea and called me. The father said, "Hey, old buddy, what would be the possibility of your taking Deborah with you on the plane? We'll call some friends in Chicago, have them meet you at the airport and take Deborah off your hands, while we drive the Volkswagen back. That will take us about five days, and we'll pick Deborah up at our friends' home. You'll only have her for four or five hours on the plane."

From a logical standpoint, it sounded fine. Flight attendants on the plane could handle anything drastic that might come along, like changing a diaper and warming the baby's bottle. It seemed like a very reasonable request. These were good friends of ours, so how could I possibly turn them down?

I had a couple of days before having to make the decision, so I said, "Let me think and pray about it." I did think and pray, and as much as I wanted to say, "Yes, I'd be happy to do it," there was a feeling within me that I should say no. I had no indication from the Bible about it; it was just a feeling. In my times with the Lord, He hadn't spoken to me from some obscure passage in Ezekiel saying, "Thou shalt not take that baby on the plane [or chariot]," but there was this inner feeling of unrest and uneasiness.

The Bible says that God is not the author of confusion, but of peace (1 Corinthians 14:33). Paul also talks about the kinds of decisions that often confront us (Romans 14). The particular situation he was talking about in this section was the matter of eating meat that had been offered at a pagan temple. Rather than saying it was right or wrong, Paul gave a principle and a guideline for life situations. He stated, "But he who doubts is condemned if he eats, because his eating is not from faith; and whatever is not from faith is sin" (Romans 14:23). However, Paul points out that there are some who can eat meat offered at pagan temples with a perfectly clear conscience, who have no qualms about it whatsoever, and for those it is perfectly all right to eat the meat. He goes on to say that the "eaters" and the "non-eaters" must not condemn one another. The Bible gives no room for judging another Christian's freedom or the lack of it.

Another way to look at this principle is to explain it as the "principle of peace," as Paul said, "Be anxious for nothing, but in everything by prayer and supplication with thanksgiving let your requests be made known to God. And the peace of God, which surpasses all comprehension, shall guard your hearts and your minds in Christ Jesus" (Philippians 4:6-7). A long time ago I gave up trying to explain "the peace of God, which surpasses all comprehension." How can you possibly explain something that you can't comprehend?

Paul also talks about the peace "ruling" in your heart (Colossians 3:15). The Greek word in this verse for rule means "to be the umpire of," calling an "out" or "safe" in a definite way.

In my heart, the Holy Spirit was saying about taking Deborah, "Out! Don't do it"; I had doubt, unrest, and no peace about taking her on that plane.

So when her parents called, very apologetically I turned them down (because I did feel like a heel about it). I could tell by the tone of their voices on the other end of the phone that they did not completely understand my decision.

That afternoon I climbed on the airplane and flew to Chicago. We got there and the field was completely fogged in. We made three passes to try to get into O'Hare, but finally the pilot announced, "Folks, we are really sorry. We have made three attempts to land at O'Hare and we are getting low on fuel. We can't wait any longer for the ceiling to lift, so we are going to take you back to Kansas City and put you up there overnight."

I had exactly seven dollars in my pocket and was flying Economy. I didn't realize till that night that when you fly Economy on some airlines, they don't pay for your hotel and food if something happens. This meant that I had to find a hotel room in Kansas City for about six dollars and fifty cents, leaving me enough for a hot dog for supper. Thoughts of having a six-month-old baby in that hotel room, out of milk, with no clean diapers, made me break out in a cold sweat.

The Lord does want to lead us in all situations. I realize that the consequences don't always turn out as dramatically as mine did, and it isn't always as clear as to the why of His leading. But the truth is that He wants to lead us. If we are willing to do anything He asks of us in a given situation, if we are willing to commit it to Him in prayer and to wait on Him, He will show us His will. And we can make good decisions that are spiritual in nature and are in accordance with His plan for us.

While it is ultimately the husband's responsiblity to make the decision, it is imperative that he listens — and really *hears* his wife's point of view and that the two come to a *mutual* agreement.

☞

They were a handsome couple — young, well-educated, intense. However, they weren't looking their best at the moment. Her eyes were brittle-bright, exposing a nervousness that skittered across the luncheon table. He looked drawn and tired.

We had been surprised to hear of their permanent return to the States from one of the most difficult mission fields in the world. But even more surprising was their story.

The reasons were multiple, of course. But one fact stood out. The wife had reservations from the beginning about going overseas, and had expressed these to her husband — but he had not listened.

If we are listening in order to understand—hearing with our heart—we will be able to put ourselves in the other's shoes and take into serious consideration that person's thoughts and feelings in making decisions. Tragically, some Christian men feel that if they have simply listened to their wife's words, they have adequately considered her viewpoint. Then they go ahead and make decisions independently.

Listening, according to Webster, means "to make a conscious effort to hear; attend closely"; but the second meaning is, "to give heed; take advice."

God calls us to be one in marriage. Some husbands know that, but somehow think they are the "one." Oneness means a lot of things, but certainly it means to be intertwined both in heart and in mind. Therefore, agreement on major decisions is essential before action is taken.

Some men may be thinking, "But then my wife could hold me back from doing what I feel God wants me to do."

God's commands do not contradict each other. God calls us to be "one flesh," to be subject to one another, to love, to prefer, to look out for the best interest of our mate. How can this be done when we take the attitude, "Well, thanks for your opinion. Now I'll do what I want to do"—or even "what I think God wants."

This area seems paradoxical. How can God ordain oneness and then give us opposite minds? How can a husband be "head" and responsible to *make* the decision and yet determine in his heart that, in order to love his wife as Christ loved the Church, decide that major decisions must be mutually agreed upon?

It is possible . . . with God. In the case of the couple who went to the mission field, the husband felt called to a tough and formidable mission field. His wife didn't feel that she had either the gifts or the capacity for it, but he refused to consider a less demanding country. When he didn't heed her feelings, she went with him as wholeheartedly as she was able because she wanted to support him. Two years later they were back home, the wife near a breakdown, the husband defeated. What could have prevented this tragedy?

I believe that prayer is the answer. Not ordinary, send-up-a-word kind of prayer, but agonizing, time-consuming, fervent prayer. Until. Until God reaches down and fills that wife's heart with His call to the same field and gives her the gifts and abilities to live there with joy. Or until the husband's heart is changed to stay home contentedly or be redirected to a less difficult field of service.

But because this husband had not listened to his wife, he didn't wait and pray until God changed her, him, or the situation. And, as a result, two people were deeply hurt.

It is the responsibility of the husband—as leader of his home—to see that problems, both generic (ones which occur over and over given the same set of circumstances) and occasional and life's major and minor decisions are thought through, and resolved, *together*. As head of the home, he is responsible for those decisions. As lover, he will rarely, if ever, make a decision that isn't mutually agreed upon.

Tough job? Yes.

But no one ever said leadership was easy!

Note
1. For more information on this topic, refer to the book by Jery White, *Honesty, Morality, and Conscience* (NavPress, 1979, 1996).

CHAPTER TWENTY-NINE

CHOOSING RESPONSIBILITY

by Jack

I am convinced that there are "seasons" to all of our lives, but perhaps a mother has more definite seasons. Her seasons may be divided in a number of ways, some being: "Before children," "Preschool children," "School children," and "After children."

Carole entered a different "season" just as we moved to a small townhouse in a new community and I began to travel frequently in my work. Because of a change in school systems, Lynn no longer came home for lunch.

Now my wife is not one to sit around watching television all day, because she is an activist. Considering these circumstances, I realized that I had to start praying for Carole in a special way. I knew that probably for the first time in her life she was going to find herself with time on her hands, which she would want to fill profitably. As we talked about it and prayed over the matter together, we began to ask God for areas of specific ministry and outreach.

In a few weeks, God led a young widow on the North Shore section of Chicago to begin doing Bible study with Carole. Soon Edy invited three or four of her friends to meet for Bible study and group discussion, women eager to grow in Jesus Christ. Carole and Edy began to teach them, not only how to grow in the Christian life but how to teach other women the same principles of discipleship. These women had friends who were eager to know Christ, and soon several other studies began. By the time we left the Chicago area in 1973, hundreds of women in the north and northwest suburbs were excited about living for Christ and studying the Bible together. These groups are being perpetuated by women in whose lives Carole and Edy had invested.

This leads us to continue with our discussion of key principles.

Principle number five—Determine your wife's gifts and capabilities and encourage her accordingly. What are your wife's gifts? Her strengths? Do you know what she enjoys and does well? Are you encouraging her along these lines to develop and use the strengths she has in whatever way God wants?

Dawson Trotman, the founder of The Navigators, used to say, "Never do anything that someone else will or can do when there is so much to be done that no one else can or will do."

Unfortunately, many men feel threatened by their wives' abilities. This attitude causes great limitations on what God wants to accomplish through that particular *couple*. God made a man and a woman to "fit together"—to complete one another—to be more effective together than either one could be alone. Some men unconsciously say, "Well, as long as my wife's gifts are mainly in the kitchen, I'll encourage her."

Now, I am glad that some of Carole's natural gifts do lie in the homemaking area, and that she is challenged by and enjoys our home. I have no difficulty at all delegating all responsibility in the areas of planning meals, shopping, cooking, and organizing for entertaining. I help when I can, but mainly all I am good for is walking through the kitchen. We sit down and talk about what we ought to do in the way of being hospitable and how we should entertain, but she has the gifts in that area and I am very glad to delegate it to her. Most men have no trouble with that.

But a number of men are intimidated if their wives get more phone calls than they do. And if their gifts happen to overlap, they get upset. Instead of figuring out how they as a couple can "fit together," this kind of man suddenly starts demanding so much in the home that his poor wife has no energy left to use other gifts—spiritual gifts—that God has given her with which to be creative.

God did not bring us together to compete with one another, but to complete one another. If a wife feels stifled, boxed in by being "just a housewife," if she does not feel she is living up to her God-given abilities, it may be because the husband is not following this principle to determine his wife's gifts and capabilities in all areas and encourage her accordingly.

Principle number six—Seek responsibility and take responsibility for your actions. Seek responsibility. Many men have abdicated their leadership and women have encouraged them to do so. Men need to take initiative in leadership. I am not talking about demanding submission; I am talking about accepting responsibility.

The second part of the guideline is just as difficult: to take responsibility for your actions. Believe it or not, there will be times when you are 100 percent wrong. You have been the worst leader and have made the worst decisions this side of Napoleon's defeat at Waterloo. Now what are you going to do? One thing only. Say, "I'm sorry. I was wrong. I will endeavor never to repeat this mistake. Will you forgive me?" and mean it!

You may have to say this to your children when you have done unkind, inconsiderate, and hurtful things.

Are you man enough to say, "I'm sorry. Will you forgive me?" A good leader seeks responsibility and is willing to accept the responsibility for his actions—when they are right *and* when they are wrong. Especially when they are wrong.

Before we finish discussing what leadership is for a husband, we need a reminder. Submission is the lifestyle of every Christian. A Christian is, first of all, to obey God. And God says His servants are to obey their spiritual leaders, the government, their parents, their elders, and each other. That just about covers the territory! We are all called on to be "subject to one another" (Ephesians 5:21), in a context that begins the commands to husbands and wives.

Please note that the command to be "subject to one another" precedes the discussion on headship and submission in Ephesians 5. That is extremely significant. God did not make a mistake in putting that statement there, nor is it incompatible with what follows. As the head of my home, I have a responsibility of serving, of submitting, of looking out for Carole and Lynn with tenderness, a giving of self that must be constant. I can never, I *must* never demand submission from my wife. It is Carole's to give—or withhold. She is commanded in a special way to be subject to me as her husband (I'm not commanded to remind her to submit to me). If she isn't, she is disobeying God, but even then that doesn't mean that I can demand it.

In summary, then, these are the principles of good leadership:

1. Know your wife in order to look out for her welfare.
2. Keep the channels of communication open and clear. See that any generic difficulties are thought through together.
3. Set an example.
4. Make sound and timely decisions.
5. Determine your wife's gifts and capabilities and encourage her accordingly.
6. Seek responsibility and take responsibility for your actions.

Headship is leadership, a leadership of love. It is not a general commanding his army, a computer analyst pushing the right buttons, a master in charge of his slave. It is simply taking our God-given responsibility to care for our wives and families and to lead them in love toward the goals which God has chosen for us.

CHAPTER THIRTY

CHOOSING TO SUBMIT

by Carole

Sunlight danced over the bedspread, reflected to the walls, and splashed on the blue carpet. Birds, perched on the telephone wire outside my window, competed for the cheeriest song of the day. But a greater contest was going on inside my soul and made me deaf to their music . . . a struggle that climaxed smaller battles fought during several weeks over the concept of submission.

Submission! How I hated that word. When it flashed into my mind, all I could conjure up was a nonentity, a nothing sort of yes-woman. I didn't want to be only a reflection of another person.

Yet here I was faced with the no-nonsense command of God: "Wives, be subject to your own husbands, as to the Lord" (Ephesians 5:22). I had argued with God and with everyone else that this verse could not mean what it looked like on the surface; that it was surely a cultural statement that had meaning only for Bible times.

In my stubborn resistance, I searched the Bible to see if there were exceptions to that command, examples of godly women who didn't submit to their husbands. I couldn't find any. Abigail came closest when she bypassed her drunken husband to take food to

David and his men when Nabal had refused (1 Samuel 25). But she did it to save her husband and the men of his household. She was obeying the command to "do him good and not evil all the days of her life" (Proverbs 31:12).

My next attempt was to reconstruct the verse to read, "Wives, submit yourselves unto your husbands as to the Lord when they are acting like the Lord." But I knew it didn't mean that.

As I searched the Word that fifth year of our marriage, I had to conclude that this verse meant I was to submit to Jack in the same free and "nothing-held-back" way that I wanted to submit to Jesus Christ.

Up to that point I had felt that marriage was a 50-50 proposition, and if Jack would give his 50 percent, I would give mine. However, it seemed that frequently we would fight to determine whose turn it was to give that 50 percent. I had yet to learn that a happy, biblical marriage is one that is a 100 percent proposition with each partner willing to give 100 percent.

That spring, God had begun a deep work in Jack's life and I saw the need for much change in my own. I asked God to deepen me and help me grow. And one of the first seeds He planted in the soil of my mind was to "submit to your husband"—to adapt to him and let him be the leader. It was a seed I would have just as soon dumped in the "throw-away" bin.

Jack, being a strong leader of people anyway, always had been the head of our home and way down inside of me I knew this and respected him because of it. But it wasn't for my lack of trying to run things that he continued his leadership. I tried every wile possible to "win."

That sunny day God faced me squarely with the need to make up my mind—was I going to obey Him or not? To obey God meant obeying Jack—when I felt like it and when I didn't feel like it; when he was loving and when he was disagreeable. It was in those "disagreeable" times that I knew I would have to do it for God's sake and not for Jack's. If Lynn didn't obey her babysitter when I had told her to, it wasn't the babysitter she was disobeying as much as me. In fact, mostly me. She might not obey for the babysitter's sake, but she needed to for my sake. The issue was clear.

God was waiting to open a closed door in my life. For me, this became a lordship decision. "If God is not Lord of all, He is not Lord at all" had been a truth I had known for years, and it was brought again to my mind. If God were not Lord of my attitudes in marriage, He was not Lord of my life because I was still making the decisions as to what parts of my life He could or could not control. I had to come to grips with this all-important question: was I willing to trust God in this area, whatever it meant? Even if it meant becoming all those things I feared most . . . a nonentity . . . a nothing? Was I willing *for God*?

Tears dropped on the pages of my Bible. After what felt like hours of inner wrestling and struggle, I finally said, "Yes, Lord. Whatever it means, I really want to submit to Jack because You say to, and I want to obey."

At the moment I took that step of submitting my will, I could not see how it would turn out well. I honestly thought Jack might become selfish, demanding, and unfair. But the exact opposite happened. When Jack saw that I wasn't fighting to get my own way, or to run his life, or to change him, he became more unselfish, more tender, less demanding. He asked my opinion on things he had never asked before. We grew closer as he included me in a greater variety of decisions, something beautiful happened in our lives.

And instead of deteriorating into a blob, I felt like I was emerging from a cocoon to stretch my wings and fly . . . and find out who I really was.

Now please don't think that I've "arrived," for I have a long way to go. I have an independent streak in me that you wouldn't believe. It still makes me want things *my* way in *my* time with *my* needs paramount. Self continues to demand, "Meet my needs." But love, God's love within me, cries, "Let me meet *your* needs."

Most of us don't want husbands we can dominate, but many

of us will try our best to get our own way. So if we can't dominate, we will maneuver. Now I am a pretty good maneuverer, but God showed me that was wrong too. To manipulate, to control, to manage are all verbs expressing the same power play.

I guess the most exciting thing I discovered was that "God's commandments are not grievous" (1 John 5:3, KJV). In other words, His commands are not to make us unhappy or to be hard on us, but to make us live life freely, fully, and joyfully.

I have been reading a number of women authors who feel that anyone who is in submission to another individual is inferior, which, if logically carried through, would mean that children are inferior to parents, younger people are inferior to older people, we are inferior to our government, and most of all, that Christ was inferior to the Father because Jesus submitted Himself to God the Father. The latter is heresy, the former foolish.

Most of these women have decided that submission is out of date, or a result of the fall, or a statement that Paul made in the flesh before he was enlightened. Interestingly, I have never read in any of these books the thought that the husband's command to "love his wife as his own body," which is in the same paragraph, is anything but literal and applicable to us today.

We must stop buying what the world is trying to sell. It will lead to heartbreak and sorrow if we pursue it.

The other extreme is to put a straitjacket on wives by binding them with the few short passages directed specifically to wives. All of Scripture is for wives. All of the Bible is for every Christian. Scriptures such as "speak the truth in love" and "admonish one another daily" are totally compatible with being a wife who is in submission to her husband (see Romans 15:14, Ephesians 4:15).

Submission is an attitude of heart . . . and an attitude of yieldedness and of love. In our family it works like this: in every decision, major or minor, I freely and openly tell Jack my opinions and feelings. If we don't agree, we come to a compromise solution 99 percent of the time. (This is not like the couple where the wife wanted a fur coat and the husband wanted a new car, so they compromised; she bought the coat, but kept it in the garage!) In a small number of cases when we can't come to a compromise, it is Jack's responsibility before God to make the final decision.

In some instances Jack decides my way because he loves me. If we have diametrically opposed views on a couch, for instance, and can't find one we both really like (which has never been the case, incidentally), Jack may buy the one I like because I have to live with it more hours of the day than he does.

However, after a full discussion of a matter if he feels before God that we must go in one direction while I feel we should go in the other, it is Jack's responsibility to make that decision. And it is my responsibility to submit to his decision . . . and get behind him in it too. God will hold the husband responsible for the decision, but he holds the wife responsible for her submission to that decision.

As I think about it, I am aware that most women do not have a problem with their husbands making the final decision if they feel that they have been truly heard and their viewpoint understood. Men, please take special note of that last sentence. Some husbands don't give their wives the opportunity to interact, to express all of their thoughts and feelings, and to be valued in those opinions. When a woman does not feel her viewpoint has been completely listened to, it is difficult for her not to be resentful when her husband makes a decision in which they are not in agreement. Of course, even in this a wife has no excuse for a bitter and resentful heart. God is in control and He will give grace to be rid of bitterness if we ask Him (Hebrews 12:15).

Wives have said to me, "If my husband would fulfill his part—to love me as Christ loves the Church—I would be more than willing to submit to him."

Of course. Then it would be so easy. But there is no verse that reads, "If the husband acts lovingly, then a wife should submit to him." Neither is there a verse that reads, "If a wife submits to her husband, then he should act lovingly." This is not a "I-will-if-you-will" situation. A husband is commanded to love his wife as Christ loved the church if she never submits to him. A wife is commanded to submit to her husband regardless of his demonstrating love for her. It is only in the 100 percent commitment to the command of God and to our mates that we are able to have harmony and peace in our marriages.

Is there no recourse? Yes, there is.

The best advice I was ever given was a few months after I determined to obey this command to submit. At a conference in Colorado, a wife said, "Whenever my husband makes a wrong decision, or does something I don't like, or whenever I see a characteristic in his life that is ugly, I do one thing." I was literally sitting on the edge of my chair in anticipation. At last I was about to learn a tremendous tool to use to change my husband, and I was all ears.

She continued, "I pray!"

I felt like someone had stuck a finger in the rising dough of my expectations and it had fallen with a thud. I thought, *Now come on, friend. You just have to do more than that.* My philosophy at that time was "faith without hints is dead."

But as she continued, my hopes began to rise again.

She said, "Inevitably when I pray, one of three things happens. First, my husband changes. God is in the business of changing people." I since have learned to keep a separate prayer list just for Jack—one he never sees. It has been exciting over the years to see the way God has answered requests on that list.

She continued, "Second, my husband asks me about the decision or problem again. I have had a chance to pray about it, think through on it, and perhaps find how to approach it in another way. God has put it in his heart to ask me again and has prepared his heart for my answer. He accepts it in a positive way and change occurs.

"Third, God lays it on my heart to bring the matter up again and share my thoughts freely. We are one. There is nothing that should come between us. God gives me the wisdom in sharing this in a positive, constructive way instead of negatively, and he accepts it."

As I began to practice her advice, I was astounded. It really worked. I found that as I prayed over the difficulties, God erased some of them completely from my heart. It was as though He said, "I'll take care of that. Leave it to Me. You won't even have to bring it up." And I could forget it. At other times, as I would pray, the worry would be wiped away, but the hard little knot of coldness remained. This became my way of knowing it was a matter I needed to bring up again at the first available opportunity. But I still had had a chance to pray and think about it, so it wasn't expressed in anger.

After a time, I added a fourth point to her list. In the area of decision making, at least in our home, Jack is generally right. When I am able to be objective about it, I see it. So, in these cases of disagreement, God changes my heart as I pray. He has saved us from a big scene and I am grateful for that.

God is helping me grow in practicing this plan, though I fail frequently. I erupt instead of praying. I have discovered that prayer does work, however, and not just with my husband. I have a feeling that Jack practices it with me too, which is a mighty good idea. Husbands can't change wives. They may be able to control them to some degree, but they can't change them. Only God can do that.

I think of this poem frequently in relation to learning submission:

> Lord, I am learning
> That marriage from first to last
> Is an adventure
> A long series of recurring "happenings"
> In which we triumph or fail.
> That when I let God be God
> When according to Your Word I joyfully submit

To my husband's authority
My sense of fulfillment
Is at high peak.
I can face life head-on
I can live with myself creatively
Not ironclad rules
But ironclad love. It works, Lord
Just as You said it would.
I am learning.[1]

Note
1. Ruth Harms Calkin, "I Am Learning," *Tell Me Again, Lord, I Forget* (Elgin, Ill.: David C. Cook Publishing Co., 1974), pp. 22-23.

PART SIX

THE PHYSICAL RELATIONSHIP

CHAPTER THIRTY-ONE

CHOOSING TO BE "ONE FLESH"

by Jack

My wife calls it "the oil in the machinery." To me, it is the "frosting on the cake." And there is no masculine/feminine contradiction.

It can be the greatest fun in all of life or more trouble and heartache than anything else in the marriage relationship. It has many names, some beautiful, some coarse. The simplest is *sex*.

When God created the human race, He made them male and female, and as God looked out over His creation, He declared, "Behold, it is *very* good" (Genesis 1:31).

Then God decreed that a husband and wife should be "one flesh," referring to sexual unity—a beautiful thing in God's eyes.

In His wonderful wisdom God designed sexual intercourse for at least three reasons: for the propagation of the human race, for the expression of the kind of love between a man and wife which nourishes true oneness, and for pleasure.

Some today have become trapped in the snares of the so-called "new morality" (which really is the old immorality with a new name) or in situation ethics. Some have bought what the world is selling in the Playboy Philosophy. Others, reacting violently to these philosophies, have landed back among the distorted images of somber, negative Puritanism.

But according to the Bible, sex is a gift from God with a wonderful purpose. The first two purposes mentioned—for the propagation of the human race and for the building of love—are generally accepted by the Christian world. Scripture passages such as Genesis 1:27-28, 9:1, and Psalm 127:3 both command and bless the propagating of the human race. God could have invented other ways for us to conceive children. He could have had us exchange ear wax with Q-Tips! It is beautiful to me that God came up with a way of promoting the human race that was so irresistible men and women can't stay away from it. He invented something so unique and delightful that the growth of the human race was ensured.

The second purpose—to promote mutual love—is shown us in the phrase "and the two shall become one flesh." This statement, found four times in Scripture (Genesis 2:24, Matthew 19:5, Mark 10:7, Ephesians 5:31), certainly has in it the aspects of emotional, spiritual, and mental oneness. But the ultimate meaning here is physical—a blending of two bodies into one flesh to promote mutual love.

Some people have more difficulty accepting the third purpose for sex, which is that it is for our enjoyment. It was given us for pure pleasure. The Scriptures that make this fact clear are often overlooked. Paul said, "But because of immoralities, let each man have his own wife, and let each woman have her own husband" (1 Corinthians 7:2). The pull of the sex drive is so great, Paul gives a warning about it to those who are unmarried and then says, "Let the husband fulfill his duty to his wife, and likewise also the wife to her husband" (7:3). Another version translates duty as "conjugal rights." Now the expression conjugal rights or duty doesn't communicate too well to me, but what this really means is that we are not to withhold the pleasure that is rightfully owed each other; we are to enjoy one another.

Sex is a God-given drive. Every God-given drive has a design in which it is to operate. For instance, hunger is a drive given to us by God. He knew that He had to do something to ensure that we eat in order to keep us alive to propagate the human race, because dead people do not reproduce. Unless there was some mechanism in us that would indicate to us, "It's time to eat; I'm hungry," some of us might starve to death. Some would be so busy, they would forget to eat entirely. (For others of us, we'd like to turn that drive off for a while so we wouldn't fight a continual "battle of the bulge.") The hunger drive is given by God, but the Scriptures are clear that this drive is to be handled within the framework or design of moderation.

Ambition is a God-given drive also, but it is also to be handled within the design of God's will. As long as we are in God's will in our jobs or in other situations and walking daily in the light of His will, there is absolutely nothing wrong with godly ambition, initiative, and creativity.

In the same way, sex is a God-given drive, designed by God to operate within the framework of marriage. Within this framework, it produces harmony, happiness, and freedom. Those who misuse this gift apart from God's design find heartache, shallowness, and anxiety. The Playboy Philosophy of "using" a woman for a plaything to gratify the desires of the flesh is diametrically opposed to God's design and program for sex.

I am emphasizing the pleasure aspect of sex because many still have problems believing God chose to delight us with this gift. Within His framework and design, sex has been given to us to enjoy. Hang-ups from our backgrounds, making us feel that sex is dirty, sinful, or shameful, have devastating effects on us and our children when they marry.

An illustration of the pleasure of sex may be found in the life of one of the great patriarchs of the faith. God had promised Abraham a son whose descendants would become as the sands on the seashore and the stars of heaven. But no son was born to Abraham and Sarah, and he was now 100 years old and she was ninety. But Abraham continued to depend on God to fulfill His promise to him and Sarah.

Finally, God sent three angels to Abraham and speaking through them said, "Where is Sarah, your wife?"

Abraham answered, "Behold, in the tent."

Then God said, "I will surely return to you at this time next year, and behold, Sarah your wife shall have a son."

"And Sarah was listening at the tent door, which was behind him. Now Abraham and Sarah were old, advanced in age; it had ceased to be with Sarah after the manner of women" (Genesis 18:12, see 18:9-11).

The last phrase, referring to "the manner of women," could mean a number of things, but the foremost meaning undoubtedly is that she could no longer conceive. A secondary meaning could be that she was no longer enjoying her husband physically.

"And Sarah laughed to herself, saying, "After I have become old, shall I have *pleasure*, my lord being old also?'" (18:12, emphasis added).

Isn't it interesting that the Spirit of God chose this word to use here? "Shall I have *pleasure*?" (This is the same Hebrew word that is used for Eden, as in "the Garden of Eden.") From the response of God in the next statement, we know that Sarah also meant the pleasure of having a son, but I really think something else was on her mind as well. It was not unusual for men of Abraham's age to father many children; indeed, he had fathered Ishmael by Hagar some years before and would have other children by Keturah after Sarah's death. Yet Sarah here mentions Abraham's age as well as her own in the sentence about having pleasure. This makes me feel that they probably weren't enjoying each other physically at that time.

They then had "pleasure," and it produced the joy of a son from their union. Isaac was born and, many years later, married Rebekah.

"So Isaac lived in Gerar. When the men of the place asked about his wife, he said, 'She is my sister,' for he was afraid to say, 'My wife,' thinking, 'The men of the place might kill me on account of Rebekah, for she is beautiful.' And it came about, when he had been there a long time, that Abimelech king of the Philistines looked out through a window and saw, and behold, Isaac was caressing his wife Rebekah" (Genesis 26:6-8).

One translation says, "Sporting with" (KJV). You may be sure they were not playing chess. "Then Abimelech called Isaac and said, 'Behold, certainly she is your wife! How then did you say, "She is my sister"?' And Isaac said to him, 'Because I said, "Lest I die on account of her"'" (Genesis 26:9).

Apparently Isaac was doing something with Rebekah that he would not do with his sister. Whatever it was, caressing, fondling, "sporting with," you may be sure they were delighting in one another.

The whole book of the Song of Solomon is a love poem between two people who are in love with one another. The Bible uses very intimate and beautiful language to describe the relationship these two lovers had (see 1:13; 4:5,10; 5:4,16).

If we have background cobwebs remaining in our minds, let us ask God for the clean purifying sweep of His Word, that we may know that not only is sex within marriage straight from the hand of God, but He gave it to us as a gift to enjoy.

CHAPTER THIRTY-TWO

CHOOSING TO UNDERSTAND SEXUAL DIFFERENCES

by Jack

Sexually, men and women are different. And anatomy is only a small part of that difference. We are diverse in our approaches, our responses, and what it means to us. Unless we understand and adjust to these variances, we are in trouble.

Here are some distinctives:

- To a man sex is a delightful intermission in the drama; to a woman it is inexorably woven into the fabric of the whole.
- The male sex drive is generated by physical needs, accompanied by emotional needs; a woman's drive stems from emotional needs, along with physical needs.
- A man thinks, *How often?* A woman ponders, *How?*
- A man's thought is reduced to the moment; a woman's to what is produced by the moment. (During intercourse, a man rarely thinks of the act resulting in a baby, while this may be much on a woman's mind.)
- A man is quick to react to stimulation; a woman, comparatively slow to react, needs to be stimulated.

■ A man is primarily stimulated by one of his senses—
sight; a woman is stimulated by all five plus one—
touch, hearing, sight, taste, and smell. (This difference
is important. A number of wives have confided to
Carole and me that they were unable to respond physically to their husbands because they smelled. Perspiration, stale smoke, and bad breath can all inhibit a
woman's enjoyment of sex. It is also true that men can
be turned off by unpleasant smells, but women seem
to be more careful about such things.) The extra "plus
one" is *tenderness*.

To summarize with an illustration: A man is like an electric
light bulb—you flip a switch and on he goes. A woman is more
like an electric iron—you flip a switch and it takes a little time
to warm up. When you turn it off, it takes a bit of time to cool
off too.

Now if you don't remember any of the other differences,
please remember that one. It is very important in learning to be a
lover. And men need to learn to be lovers if they are to satisfy the
needs of their wives.

I get discouraged sometimes when I talk with some
men about their pattern in making love. Some have the lovemaking instincts of a frog, and maybe I'm being disrespectful
to a frog!

Note this often typical situation. He gets home from work and
gives her a little peck on the cheek. They have supper. He sits
down and relaxes, reads the paper, watches some television, then
it is bedtime. So he goes into the bathroom, does his little chores,
and gets into his pajamas. She does the same thing and they climb
in bed. They read a little while, perhaps, then she reaches over
and turns off her light. He reads a few minutes longer, and finally
reaches over and turns off his light. All is quiet.

And then, suddenly, out of the dark . . . comes a hand.

What a romantic setting! What psychological buildup! What creative imagination! Like I said, "All the instincts of a frog!"

Now, men, we can do better than that.

One time, a month after we had presented this subject to a group at a seminar, I ran into one of the women who had attended. She smiled and said, "You know, now my husband on occasion will call in the afternoon from the office and as we are chatting will say, 'By the way, honey, will you please turn on the iron.'"

She was excited about that.

If a man has a desire to make love that evening and has it on his mind all day just waiting to get home that night, but his wife doesn't know anything about it, and he pulls that "hand in the dark" routine, if she can respond with enthusiasm, then he has a very unusual wife.

On the other hand, if as he leaves the house in the morning, he gives her a very warm kiss and communicates in their own secret little code that he is looking forward to some fun that night, it will turn up her thermostat just a bit and it will stay warm all day long. By the time he gets home, the atmosphere has already been created and the two are far more likely to have a wonderful time that night.

Now what I have written may not apply to everyone. We are all unique individuals. But think, then talk together about your needs and ideas to promote greater mutual enjoyment in your sex lives. If you want an "angel in the home and a tigress in bed," you must communicate what excites and pleasures you.

Have you ever discussed the degree of dress or undress that stimulates desire? Or the kind of apparel? Some men who don't like black nightgowns have not said so, and their wives have been buying black nightgowns for years with the mistaken notion that their husbands found them sexy.

Those of us who have been married some years hopefully have gotten courageous enough to walk into the lingerie department of a large store and bravely walk up to the counter (as though we do it every day of the week) and say, "I'll take one of those." The "those" is something that she will wear only for you, a gesture of love and appreciation, but also something that will excite you.

May God deliver us from the "hand in the dark" approach. We need to use our imaginations and our creativity to set the mood for our lovemaking. Sex should be fun. And variety will enhance that fun.

Have you ever used your imagination to create a whole other world for your lovemaking? Your imagination can transport you out of that bedroom and the monotony of its four walls, so that you can journey together to a desert island where you are marooned with no rescue in sight, or a little cabin, snowbound after skiing all day. Imagining wholesome situations, various times, diverse places, all can add to your enjoyment together.

Good ideas can also be obtained from many marriage manuals, but many couples read the wrong ones or too many of them. They get so wrapped up in the "ideal," that they become totally unreal. Many manuals, for instance, hold that the epitome of the sex relationship is to have a climax together. This can be like a carrot held out to a bunch of racing rabbits—always just out of reach. As long as both are enjoying the physical relationship and both are usually reaching a climax, it just isn't that important to reach it together. The enjoyment is the primary concern. And the climax will not be the same every time. I have talked to people who think that unless they have the greatest, most exciting feeling in their lives each time, they are disappointed. It is always exciting—or should be. It is always thrilling, but it is never the same.

One of my favorite meals is a steak, baked potato, rolls, and apple pie. That is a real banquet for me. But I also like McDonald's hamburgers. In fact, I'm crazy about McDonald's hamburgers. And I am satisfied with either the steak dinner or a McDonald's hamburger.

That is sort of the way it is with sex. Sometimes it's like the steak, baked potato, rolls, and apple pie. At other times, it's just like McDonald's hamburgers. But it is always great. And it satisfies my needs and hers.

I hope you are reading this aloud and together as a couple. And that this will cause you to stop and talk about the whole area of the physical union, which is probably the most neglected area of communication between husbands and wives. It needs to be talked about at length, prayed over, and experienced together so that in a more full way each year, the two of you will truly become "one flesh."

CHAPTER THIRTY-THREE

CHOOSING THE BEST

by Carole

We drove along in silence for several miles. I could tell by the minuscule frown on her face that she was thinking deeply. The conversation had turned to marriage and it was obvious that this wife of several years had a problem. As we left the city and the traffic thinned, she took a deep breath and said, "But how can I really keep my marriage exciting? Ours is a good marriage. We love each other. But somehow the fun, excitement, and sparkle have faded from our relationship. Is it possible to really keep the excitement in a marriage?"

As we talked, it became apparent that she had stopped doing a great many little things she had done at first. She didn't greet her husband at the door any more with a smile and a kiss; she and her husband had stopped dating when the children came; someone else now took him to the airport for his trips and picked him up. But mainly it was their sex life that had become routine and dull. When the fun of sex evaporated into monotony, the little private jokes between them disappeared, and the electricity generated by both was cut off and no "sparks" remained. Exit excitement.

A unique, exciting physical relationship does not just happen. As in other areas of our marriages, it has to be worked at and planned for.

A woman has a difficult time separating love and sex. They are intertwined clear down to her inner being. At times a woman longs much more for the closeness and intimacy of the sex act than she does for the thrill of it. Most women long to be held, totally apart from sex. Understanding husbands need to be aware of the need for closeness that many wives have.

God has depths in the sexual area of our lives that few of us will ever plumb. It is difficult sometimes to keep God's perspective in a world that tries continually to make sex into one of the better body functions. One article to college students pointed out that it shouldn't hurt any more to break up after a fellow and girl had slept together than if they hadn't had intercourse. After all, the article said, it is just another body function. How sad! The shallowness of this point of view is leaving frustrated and despairing people in its wake.

God's plan is for sex to be like a deep, refreshing well, with water that keeps springing up—invigorating, refreshing, pure. Solomon teaches us that when we make God's gift of sex impure, in other words, when we commit adultery and fornication, it is like stagnant, shallow water on the streets of our lives (see Proverbs 5:15-19).

Do we want the "muddy puddles" of casual sex or the "deep wells" which exist within the marriage relationship? We can't have it both ways. And the choice is ours. God will give us the deep wells to refresh our spirits and our bodies, wells that can be more beautiful with passing years. God wants a growing depth in our relation together, and this is a "bottomless" well as far as I am concerned. One that can keep being explored with depths never reached. It has been said, "Sex is not something you do. Sex is something you are becoming together." And this is true.

Sex never needs to be boring or routine. God created us with a desire which is much like taking a long, cold drink of water on a hot summer afternoon. "Let your fountain be blessed, and rejoice in the wife of your youth. As a loving hind and a graceful doe, let her breasts satisfy you at all times; be exhilarated always with her love" (Proverbs 5:18-19).

Our God is a creative God. He can give us creative ideas in our sex lives. Do you ever pray for creativity from God in this area? You may. Do you ever pray that you will be a blessing to your mate in your physical relationship? You may. Do you ever ask God for His point of view when you experience hang-ups from your childhood? Do. God is interested in all our problems including those we have in this area.

One Old Testament phrase for intercourse is *to know*. "Adam knew Eve his wife; and she conceived" (Genesis 4:1, KJV). This is a beautiful word because, to me, sex is total communication — body, soul, spirit. Total knowledge completes communication.

That's what it should be, but often isn't.

Probably one of the first things a couple needs to do is to know and understand the facts. Many people have a terrible time just speaking out loud the correct name for parts of the body. Then they wonder why it is difficult for them to communicate about intimate areas of sex.

So, if you have never done it before, read a good marriage manual on sex aloud and together. Herbert Miles' *Sexual Happiness in Marriage*, Tim and Beverly LaHaye's *The Act of Marriage*, and Ed and Gaye Wheat's *Intended for Pleasure* are excellent and from a Christian point of view. Dr. Ed Wheat has also produced tapes that give a medical doctor's perspective.

Engaged couples should be encouraged to read these books separately during the engagement period, and then aloud together a week or so before they are married. If they do this, it will enable them to begin to communicate in an area where so many can't get the words out of their throats.

It is hard to believe that in this day of sex instruction in schools, on television, and in the movies, sex is still the number one matter couples have trouble talking about. Free and open discussion is essential. It is the first step on the road to "Excitement."

CHAPTER THIRTY-FOUR

CHOOSING TO GIVE

by Carole

One summer four women came to me within a week with problems that I thought were unusual at the time, but now know to be quite common. As they shared their experiences, I discovered that God had foreseen the difficulties and written down the answers many years ago. The Bible is the best marriage manual in existence and it has many practical answers to sexual problems. It shouldn't surprise us that the inventor of marriage knows how to handle the difficulties, but sometimes the Bible is the last place we look for solutions.

The first woman had been married a number of years, but had never experienced a climax. The second was married to a man who so repulsed her, she couldn't stand to have him come near her. The third, a young woman married for two years, was so shy that she was afraid of undressing in the same room with her husband. And the fourth woman said that her husband hadn't come near her in four years (this was not a case of impotency due to alcohol or to some other physical problem).

The solution to all four problems is condensed into one word: *obedience*. Obedience, not to husband or to wife, but to God Himself.

Does that sound too simple? Oh, that it were! The two things that are necessary are having God's perspective on the whole idea of sex and being committed to obeying God in that perspective.

Remember, while God doesn't give us chapters of the Bible detailing answers to sexual problems, He does give us commands that insure a healthy, beautiful physical relationship. And when He gives a command, He will give the wisdom, insight, and strength to us to obey that command if we are willing to do so. God's principles are found in a part of Paul's first letter to the Corinthians:

> The husband should give his wife what is due to her as his wife, and the wife should be as fair to her husband. The wife has no longer full rights over her own person, but shares them with her husband. In the same way the husband shares his personal rights with his wife. Do not cheat each other of normal sexual intercourse, unless of course you both decide to abstain temporarily to make special opportunity for prayer. But afterwards you should resume relations as before, or you will expose yourselves to the obvious temptation of Satan. (1 Corinthians 7:3-8, PH)

Does that teaching still sound too simple? If only we could have God's perspective on our physical problems. If only we could understand how a great many of our sexual difficulties are because we are selfish . . . we want to get instead of giving.

Notice in the chart on page 230 how specifically God's principles from this passage answer the problems of the four wives that I listed earlier.

God will enable and help us figure out the answers to the "why" and "what-to-do-about-it" questions. We need to do two things. First, pray, and then communicate to our mates about our problems. I am not suggesting that the wife whose husband repulses her say, "Hey, you are repulsive to me. I can't stand your touch." (She would never have to be repulsed again, but she wouldn't have a husband either.) But she may need to say, "You know, I am not responding to you physically in the way that I know you want me to and the way I want to. Let's talk about it and pray about it together."

GOD'S VIEWPOINT AND COMMAND:	ANSWER TO:
Do not cheat each other of normal sexual intercourse.	The wife who never had experienced orgasm *is* being cheated of normal sexual intercourse and needs to ask God for a wise counselor to help find the reason.
Neither husband nor wife have "full rights" over their own persons, but share them. Their bodies belong to each other. Before God, they are one and unashamed.	The wife repulsed by her husband—how can she be repulsed by a part of herself?
	The wife afraid to undress in the same room with her husband does not need to feel shame.
The husband and wife are not to withhold from each other.	The husband who hadn't come near his wife in four years. His sin is against God as well as against his wife.

The paragraph in 1 Corinthians not only has the generic solution to the problems of these four wives, but it has many other suggestions for us to consider. Paul says that we are not to withhold sex from one another or we may expose ourselves to temptation (7:5). If we couple this with the words of Jesus, "It is inevitable that stumbling blocks come; but woe to that man through whom the stumbling block [temptation] comes" (Matthew 18:7), we see some significant truth. Wives . . . and husbands . . . are no doubt the single greatest cause of temptation for their partners. And many are not even aware of it. God says you are absolutely wrong to punish your spouse by withholding yourself sexually. This can cause problems of temptation, and the Bible says woe to you if you are the cause. God calls it sin.

Wives seem to have a special problem with this withholding, perhaps unconsciously. If a husband has been grouchy all day, snapping at his wife and children, blaming her for the flat tire he had, his hard day at the office, and his upset stomach, and then wants to make love at bedtime, his wife suddenly refers to her splitting headache.

Maybe she really does have a headache as a result of the miserable day. At other times, however, the headache is a conscious or unconscious rejection—a punishment for his ill treatment of her.

Love and sex are intertwined in the make-up of a woman. It is sometimes impossible to "turn on" physically at night if conflicts have not been resolved. Yes, impossible! Well, impossible for a woman, but not for God. Jesus said, "With God all things are possible" (Matthew 19:26).

From a man's vantage point, he must understand that a wife desperately needs tenderness, understanding, and love. To give herself freely to him, she needs to talk about those conflicts and have them solved before making love. But a wife has to realize, too, that even when her husband is ugly and unloving and the problem is still unresolved, it is wrong for her to strike back by withholding her love sexually.

Unless both are willing to give even when they don't feel like giving, friction will result. Let's suppose that within the first year or two of marriage, a couple has developed a good sex life together.

A marriage relationship with a happy sex life might be illustrated something like the diagram on page 232. If the sex life of a married couple is happy, it is a small fraction of the total relationship—perhaps 5 percent. But if it is unhappy, it colors everything else and becomes closer to 90 percent of the relationship because it affects many other parts of life.

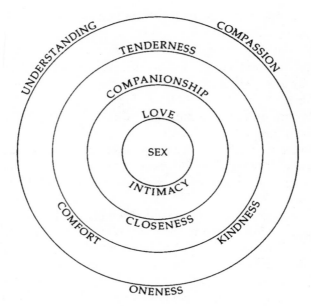

Let's develop the illustration of a couple with an unhappy sex life further.

One month the husband changes jobs, his new boss starts criticizing his work, his nerves get on edge, and he comes home irritable and unhappy. In fact, he's downright belligerent and takes his frustrations out on his wife. That night he really needs comfort and consolation and so that hand reaches out in the dark—he wants her.

But she can't . . . or won't . . . respond. She murmurs, "Not tonight."

Now this strikes at the very heart of his person, which is where she meant for it to strike. He has hurt her and she is hitting back.

Now what happens?

The next day, his attitude is ugly at work and terrible at home. Things go from bad to worse. He wants to make love again that night, but this time his wife turns him down with vehemence.

So the day after that the husband is so low that he has to reach up to touch bottom. And the vicious cycle continues downward.

If a divorce occurs, the sex life (or lack of it) may get blamed. But the primary cause in this case was allowing bad attitudes to affect the sex life. These attitudes "strip the gears" in people's lives. This is why I like to call sex the "oil in the machinery."

The building up of problems, such as the ones just described, would make the relationship diagram look something like this:

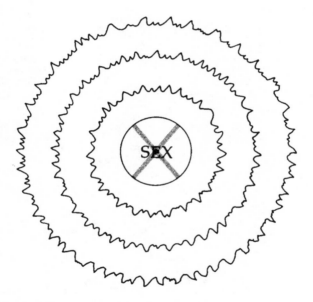

However, if a wife can say in response to her husband's desire (even when he has been a bear all day), "Lord, You know how hard it is for me to respond . . . or even want to respond to him. He has been just awful all day. I am having a hard time forgiving him, let alone forgetting and responding to him. But for You, Lord, and for our love and marriage, I want to be able to respond in love. Help me." God will help.

And in responding with love, the oil in the machinery of life will smooth out his worries and bind his hurts. Your "feast of love" may result in an opportunity to talk out the frustrations resulting in a smoothing out of the marriage relationship and a deeper, more loving oneness will result.

This would make the relationship diagram look something like this:

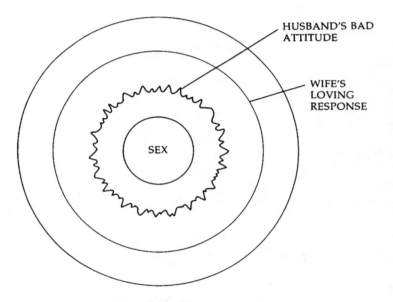

We can never build a happy marriage on resentful attitudes. It will take a miracle touch from God to turn a bitter attitude to one of forgiveness and love. But our God is a miracle-working God, and His power can create a new attitude in our hearts, if we will only ask Him for it.

CHAPTER THIRTY-FIVE

CHOOSING
TO EXPLORE

by Carole

S he wasn't just pretty, she was beautiful, one of the most attractive women I have ever met: lovely features, perfect figure, and an outgoing personality. At the moment, her beauty was marred by a red nose and puffy eyes as she told her story.

"Several years ago I heard you talk on how important it is for wives to let their husbands know they are wanted," she began, "but I didn't listen. I had never turned my husband down when he wanted to make love, but I was never all that eager for it either. However, we had a good marriage and I thought we were quite happy. Then my world collapsed. He had an affair with a woman at work—a woman who isn't even pretty. But she let him know that she was attracted to him and wanted him, and he couldn't resist her."

She twisted her handkerchief into a tiny ball and dabbed at her eyes. "Please feel free to tell my story," she continued. "I don't want anyone to go through the hell that I've known. I know now that husbands need to be wanted."

Her husband was a Christian, though not a strong one. What he had done was sin . . . against the Lord and against his wife. If he had asked, God would have given him the strength to resist the temptation and to take the "way of escape," which is promised for every testing (1 Corinthians 10:13). But this wife knew that part of the blame was hers as well. Her husband had a need that she was not fulfilling, and while she had learned of that need in time to save her marriage, heartache and scars remained.

The book of Proverbs describes a godly wife like this: "The heart of her husband doth safely trust in her, so that he shall have no need of spoil" (31:11, KJV). The spoil from war often consisted of riches and female slaves. I wonder if this is saying that a godly wife so satisfies her husband's needs that he has no longing for the power of wealth and desire for other women. *The Living Bible* paraphrases that verse, "She will richly satisfy his needs."

An article Jack and I read early in our marriage stated that most men want three different functions from the women they marry. They want a wife, a mother, and an exciting companion in bed. (This article said a "mistress," but that could be misunderstood. Jack says "tigress," and that communicates much better.)

With God's help, a woman can be all three.

When a man is sick, hurt, defeated, he needs the mother-type—to comfort, tend his hurts, and nurse his ills. Most of the time he needs a wife who is a companion, friend, idea-bouncer, encourager, helpmeet. In bed, he wants a creative woman, who is fun and who wants him.

A few men may be threatened if a wife takes an aggressive role and this whole area needs to be talked about together. But the majority of men want a woman to need them, to want them sexually.

The man needs to know he is important enough to be desired, wonderful enough to be exciting, able enough to bring a woman to heights no one else can. It is up to the wife to convince her husband that he is of inestimable value both as a lover and as a man . . . to reach out to him and let him know how great is her love and desire for him.

Way down in the depths of a man's soul lies a longing . . . a longing to be wanted . . . a need to be wanted. A loving wife will see that need and meet it with joy.

CHAPTER THIRTY-SIX

CHOOSING FAITHFULNESS

by Jack

Hearing your name paged at the airport between flights on your way home from a long-distance trip is scary. I answered the page with trepidation.

It was a longtime friend of mine. "Jack, I'm here at the airport and I need to see you."

After arranging to meet him at our departing gate, I closed my eyes and breathed a prayer for wisdom. I had talked to my friend's wife two weeks earlier and heard the pain in her voice as she told of her husband's walking out on her, the family, and the church he pastored. He left with a married woman who had been serving as the church secretary.

Several minutes later I spotted him coming toward me — and emerging from the crowd along with him was the "other woman."

Carole and I spent the better part of the next three days doing everything we could to help these two people see the awfulness of what they were doing; to see the situation from God's point of view. But we failed. Our friend did go back to his wife for a short time, but even as he left me to head home, we knew it wouldn't work. He had not repented before God but had made up his mind he wanted his lover above everyone else. Though he went through some motions to seek counsel and get further help, he had already pre-determined his course. Today he and the former church secretary are together—at the cost of two broken families, a son who has tried suicide, children who need the pieces put back together for them, a devastated church, and disgrace mantled on God's community.

This man used all the excuses that are prevalent today. Prevalent—and wrong!

"But it must be God's will," he said. "God wouldn't have put her in a place where I'd fall in love with her otherwise."

And yet he could quote by heart the Scripture:

> When tempted, no one should say, "God is tempting me." For God cannot be tempted by evil, nor does he tempt anyone; but each one is tempted when, by his own evil desire, he is dragged away and enticed. Then, after desire has conceived, it gives birth to sin; and sin, when it is full-grown, gives birth to death. (James 1:13-15, NIV)

How many times I've heard that phrase, "It has to be God's will." And even, "God told me to do it."

This is said by the very people who have sometimes preached on 1 Thessalonians 4:3-8 (NIV), which says plainly:

> It is God's will that you should be sanctified [holy]: that you should avoid sexual immorality; that each of you should learn to control his own body in a way that is holy and honorable, not in passionate lust like the heathen, who do not know God; and that in this matter no one should wrong his brother or take advantage of him. The Lord will punish men for all such sins, as we have already told you and warned you. For God did not call us to be impure, but to live a holy life. Therefore, he who rejects this instruction does not reject man but God, who gives you his Holy Spirit.

That last verse in the Phillips version says, "It is not for nothing that the Spirit God gives us is called the Holy Spirit." I like that!

My pastor friend was violating several commands from this passage alone. He was not being holy, he didn't avoid sexual immorality, he wronged a brother, he rejected God's instruction, and in a very real sense violated God's Holy Spirit. Yet he had the audacity to stand there and say, "It must be God's will."

What has happened that so many are compromising with sin, disobeying God, seeming to turn their backs on all they have taught and lived for?

I don't have all the answers to that. The pressures of the age we live in are great. We, as a nation and as individuals, have moved away from what we once saw as sin—what *is* sin. Oh, now we call it by nicer names. A person is no longer promiscuous but "sexually active." A homosexual has a different "preference." Abortion is "freedom of choice." And some would excuse adultery as God's will. Our Lord God must shudder!

When did we forget that God never said we must be happy? He said we must be obedient. He never said we'd have our fleshly desires satisfied. He told us to flee temptation, to resist the lusts of this world.

Thousands of years ago, Saul's kingdom was taken from him because of one act of disobedience. And when he tried to plead and make excuses, the prophet Samuel said, "Has the LORD as much delight in burnt offerings and sacrifices as in obeying the voice of the LORD? Behold, to obey is better than sacrifice, and to heed than the fat of rams" (1 Samuel 15:22). Today we might paraphrase that verse, "To obey God is better than what we call happiness here and now; to heed His voice is better than satisfying the most intense desire of your flesh."

But somehow we think God is going to deal with our sin less harshly than He has in days gone by. We have been duped into thinking that the most important thing in our lives is to satisfy ourselves rather than to obey Him. Somehow we make light of heaping disgrace on His bride, His Body—the Church of Jesus Christ.

So what can we do to ensure emotional and physical faithfulness for the rest of our life?

Don't play with fire or you will surely get burned. Did you know this common saying comes from the Bible? Proverbs 6:27-28 (NIV) cautions, "Can a man scoop fire into his lap without his clothes being burned? Can a man walk on hot coals without his feet being scorched?"

Be tough on yourself on this one. Today we seem to think we can flirt with temptation with immunity. And that just isn't so!

I have a friend—a former "peace child" from the sixties—who used to say often, "Oh, that's so straight," as though that were a disgusting thing to be. As she grew in the Lord, she concluded that what she was calling "straight," God called obedience. Proverbs uses this word *straight* concerning temptation: "Let your eyes look directly ahead, and let your gaze be fixed straight in front of you. . . . Do not turn to the right nor to the left; turn your foot from evil" (4:25,27).

A godly friend of mine told of walking down the street in a foreign city where he knew no one. A beautiful girl walked by him and gave him a flirtatious look. He smelled her perfume, was aware of her beauty and her availability. And he knew if he looked back, he'd fall into sin.

So he refused to look back.

It's the second look, the second thought, the second conversation, after you are aware of how pleasing the first one is, that entices. So if you are determined to obey God in being faithful to your marriage vows, consider this advice:

Know yourself and your own limits. Put up boundaries around your heart and behavior that protect the ground reserved only for your spouse. Carole and I are careful to share our deepest feelings, needs, and difficulties with each other, not with friends of the opposite sex. If a friendship with someone of the opposite sex is meeting needs that your mate should be meeting, end it now, because whether you admit it or not you are playing with fire.

We have seen great unhappiness and harm caused to a marriage when one partner becomes emotionally involved with another person, even when it doesn't lead to physical involvement. And emotional involvement is such a subtle temptation that it creeps up from one's blind side unless we are aware and open to the voice of the Holy Spirit.

Ruth Senter wrote about her encounter and ensuing friendship with a Christian man she met in a graduate class. She told of her struggle and finally her godly response to this temptation as she wrote a letter ending the relationship in which she said, "Friendship is always going somewhere unless it's dead. You and I both know where ours is going. When a relationship threatens the stability of commitments we've made to the people we value the most, it can no longer be."[1]

Realize the power of your eyes. Your eyes, it's been said, are the windows to your heart. Pull the shades down if you sense someone is pausing a little too long in front of your windows . . . reserve the deep type of look for only one person.[2]

Remember to fear God! Yes, He is a God of love and compassion. Yes, He forgives. But it is important to fear God. The fear of God is often a deterrent in my life to sin. Frankly, I'm afraid of the consequences of my sin because God says that I'll reap what I sow. And I'll do it in this life.

God is not a benign entity who overlooks sin. He is holy, and He will discipline us because He loves us.

Have you already fallen? Go to the Father and confess your disobedience. Let Him wrap His arms of love and forgiveness around you. But remember, repentance is more than words. It includes words in the form of confession, but it also includes actions that "prove" the sincerity of that confession, that create a track record to encourage trust. Paul stated it clearly in Acts 26:20: "Prove your repentance by your deeds." Jesus emphasized the same issue in Luke 3:8: "Produce fruit in keeping with repentance." If you've been unfaithful, the scars will remain but the wound can heal. It may take months, even years, but God can rebuild the waste places if you will let Him.

His is a promise that rings through time and eternity, "Now to Him who is able to keep you from stumbling, and to make you stand in the presence of His glory blameless with great joy, to the only God our Savior, through Jesus Christ our Lord, be glory, majesty, dominion and authority, before all time and now and forever. Amen" (Jude 24-25).

He can keep you from falling.

He can even keep you from stumbling!

Trust Him, and there you will find "great joy."

Notes
1. Ruth Senter, "Rick," *Partnership* (January-February 1988), quoted in *My Soapbox* (October 10, 1988).
2. Dennis Rainey, *My Soapbox* (October 10, 1988), newsletter published by Family Ministry, P.O. Box 23840, Little Rock, AR 72221-3840.

PART SEVEN

CONCLUSION

CHAPTER THIRTY-SEVEN

CHOOSING MARRIAGE

by Carole

The package was on the dining room table when I walked in the door. I stared at it blankly for a full minute before the pieces fit as to how it got there and who had sent it. Then I sat down and cried for five minutes. Tears of joy and thanksgiving.

Jack was overseas . . . an extended trip that made it impossible for him to be home on our twenty-seventh wedding anniversary. We hadn't discussed it much, but it was understood that we would celebrate on his return. But there, resplendent in white paper and giant bow, was a gift from him accompanied by a love-filled card written before he left.

He had secretly arranged with a friend, who had a key to our home, to surprise me on our anniversary. After I stopped crying, I opened the package to find a beautiful travel bag—Jack's way of saying, "I hope you can go with me next time."

Jack has grown increasingly more thoughtful over the years. I spent the next hour staring out into the sunshine mulling over memories of past anniversaries.

Oh, that marriage was always like that!

Shortly before the trip, I had rushed into the house after a fast game of tennis, all warm and moist with perspiration, makeup completely gone. Jack had been working at home all morning and was in a hurry to get back to the office, so I paused to fix him lunch before getting cleaned up. As I kissed him goodbye, I said, "I promise to look better when you get home."

He answered absently, "Why, are you going to get your hair done this afternoon?"

I howled. "I've just had my hair done . . . yesterday," I replied.

He looked sheepish, grinned weakly, and hastily retreated.

Marriages are made of such happenings. The beautiful, the irritating, the routine, the humorous, the difficult, the dramatic.

Marriage is an enormous enigma, a colossal conundrum. It is agonizing adjusting, pain and pleasure, delight and demands. It is a mixture of the mundane, the ecstatic, the commonplace, the romantic. It comes in waves, ripples, bubbles, and splashes. Its days contain thunder, sunlight, hail, wind, rain. Its hues are the rainbow's spectrum, but prominent are shades of red, purple, yellow, and gray. It is intimacy, distance, closeness, separateness. It is a quiet melody, an earthy novel, an obscure mystery, the greatest show on earth.

It is choices. Choosing to love, to understand, to enjoy, to know. It is choosing . . . marriage.

To this we attest. It is so much more fun living it than writing about it! So we are done with the writing.

Discussion Questions For Better Communication

The following questions can be used to gain knowledge of each other whether you are engaged, newly married, or even "old married folk." In order for your discussion to be most profitable, set apart some time for exploring feelings; then take a section that intrigues you and travel new roads of adventure, penetrating unexplored territory of your minds and hearts. Use the questions to search, observe, analyze, and probe new vistas.

The questions in this section are partly ours and partly adapted from Joseph B. Henry's *Fulfillment in Marriage* (Westwood, N.J.: Fleming H. Revell, 1966), pp. 56-79.

If there are difficult areas of communication in your marriage, begin with the easy topics . . . and use only the positive questions at first. Then progress to the topics you have problems discussing, and finally to those questions that may be painful but are imperative to explore. Begin with prayer . . . end with prayer. Let God be the third Person sitting in on these dialogues. And remember, *with God all things are possible.*

Communication

1. On a scale from 1 to 10 (with 10 being high), how would you rate me as a communicator? What would help me be a more effective communicator with you?
2. How free do you feel to share your fears, feelings, superstitions, opinions with me? What do I do that might make you hesitant to share these with me?
3. What words, manners of speech, phrases, tones of voice annoy you?
4. In what areas do you feel we may not be completely honest with each other, and how can we remedy this?
5. What do you see as the difference between argument and discussion? Am I more likely to argue or discuss with you? With other people?
6. How soon and in what way should we handle small problems that come up daily?
7. How do you feel when I make a suggestion for change? How can I better make these suggestions? (Or can I?)
8. Does it bother you when I ask, "What do you mean?" If so, why?
9. When and on what subjects do you feel I can be stubborn and resistant to your point of view? How can we remedy this?
10. Do you feel generally that I am thinking with you or disagreeing?
11. Can you share ideas with me freely with the feeling that I will understand you? Do you think I face facts realistically?
12. Do you feel our silent communication is good? Do I express myself by body language, facial expression, nods, gestures, or just thought waves—whether we are in a group or it's just the two of us? How could we improve on this "language without words"?

Backgrounds and Balance

1. In what areas do you feel that we are equals? Unequal?
2. How would you describe the role of a man? Of a woman?
3. How well do you feel your parents related to one another? What would you like to carry over from them? Avoid?
4. Is there any difference in our educational backgrounds that bothers you?
5. What differences in our social backgrounds might cause us conflict? Are there social habits, practices, and manners that I have that bother you? Are there some things you feel are important that I am failing to do? (Opening doors, greeting you when you arrive home, etc.)
6. What are your ideas on integration? How would you feel if a child of ours married someone of another race?

7. What do you consider our areas of mutual interest? What would be interesting and fun to develop together?

8. How do you like men/women to dress? What are some suggestions you have about the way I dress?

9. Do you think economy or quality is more important?

10. What do you like to read? What areas do we have in common in reading? Do you like to read aloud together? Is this something we should do?

11. What kind of humor do you enjoy?

12. What problem areas might we have in the way I spend money? The way you do? What would you economize on that I might not? Do you feel we can talk about these matters regularly without getting angry?

13. In your opinion, are our tastes similar or dissimilar? (In clothes, furniture, residences, sports, reading, hobbies, activities.) If not, in what areas, and does it matter to us? What can we do about this? What about our taste in cars? Size of bed? Art? Music? Magazines?

14. Who should be responsible for various aspects of the maintenance of the home? In what areas should there be division of responsibility?

15. Who do you feel should manage the money in our family?

16. Do you like to operate on a budget?

17. What do you think about mothers working outside the home?

18. What is your thinking on how much we should give from our income? What are your current areas of giving?

19. Do you like to have a savings plan? How important is it to you to save some money regularly?

20. What do you think about borrowing? From the family? From others?

21. Can we agree on a budget and each of us stick to it?

Health

1. How much do you like to exercise? How much would you like for me to exercise? Is this important to you?

2. Do you have regular medical checkups?

3. How much fresh air do you like at night?

4. Are you a slow riser? (Should I learn not to speak to you before breakfast?)

5. Is there anything in your family's medical history or in your own that I should be aware of?

6. How important is relaxation to you? How do you relax best? How can I help you in this?

Ethics

1. Do you think that most people are honest? Do you feel that it is honest or dishonest to fudge on income taxes, a child's age at a ticket window, about import duty?
2. Does it disturb you not to pay a bill on time? How important is it to you to have a good credit rating with everyone?
3. Do you regularly violate any traffic regulations? Which ones?
4. Do you feel I often exaggerate? Does this bother you?
5. How do you feel about keeping promises?
6. How do you feel about playing "tricks" on people?

Children

1. Do you want children? How many?
2. How soon would you want a child after marriage?
3. What are your thoughts about birth control and planning or spacing of children?
4. If we couldn't have children, how would you feel about that?
5. How do you feel about adoption? Foster care?
6. What are your thoughts on the discipline and training of children?
7. What changes would you make from your own childhood that relate to raising a family?
8. What are your ideas on working at being a good parent? (How can we best go about it? How important is it?)

Family Policies

1. What differences have you noted in our backgrounds? Can we face these differences honestly and adjust to one another?
2. What are the family customs from your own upbringing that you would like to continue in our family? How important is this to you?
3. Do you like to entertain? How much would you like it to be a part of our life? What sort of entertaining (casual, formal) do you prefer?
4. What are your thoughts on visiting parents and other relatives? On their visiting us?
5. What do you think about family anniversaries, birthdays, special occasions? What about gifts for these? How much would you spend on these gifts?
6. Do you feel you can be in close fellowship with your family and also be free to live your own life? Do you feel we have achieved this? In what areas do we need to work at this?

7. Do you think I do my share of work—at home and to produce income?
8. Do you feel we are in agreement about meal schedules, table practices, bedtimes, hours of sleep, house temperatures, how to spend weekends?
9. What do you think about "dating"? How important in your priorities is this time with me?
10. What do you think about a husband and wife having time away from their children? How often?
11. Do you like pets? What kind? Do you feel they should be kept outdoors?
12. If one of our parents were widowed or sick, what do you feel is our responsibility toward him/her?

Recreation and Leisure

1. What do you think is the greatest way to spend a vacation? What is your second choice?
2. Do you like to travel? Camp out?
3. Do you like to go on vacations just with us or with other people? Who do you think would be a fun couple to spend a vacation with?
4. Do you like my friends? Who would you like to spend recreation time with?
5. What are your hobbies? How much time do you like to spend on them?
6. How much time do you think should be spent watching television? What are your favorite programs? What about going to movies? Do you have personal guidelines as to the rating?
7. What kinds of sports do you like? (Playing or watching.)
8. What other kinds of things do you like? (Games, for example.)
9. Do you feel a need to be busy, or do you enjoy just "being lazy"?

Habits

1. Do you think I am inclined to be overly neat or overly sloppy? What habits would you like for me to change? Do these things bother you: unwashed dishes, unmade beds, towels not hung well, papers in stacks, papers not stacked neatly, artwork not hanging straight, and other similar things? What specifically?
2. Do I have any personal idiosyncrasies or practices that annoy you? Do you think you can accept living with these if I cannot change? (The most often mentioned are: picking teeth, sounds in eating,

spitting, scratching, twitching, snoring, sniffling, use of gum, use of tobacco, personal grooming, use of alcoholic beverages, use [or non-use] of colognes or perfumes, bathing and toilet practices, body odors, being chronically late, not hanging up clothes in the proper place, scattering belongings, not closing doors or drawers, offensive language, not replacing lids or caps, leaving the bathroom in a mess, mannerisms of speech, perverted humor, off-beat ideas, overmeticulousness, messiness, lack of organization, prudishness, artificiality.)

Spiritual Things
1. What is your concept of God? Christ? Sin? Man's relationship to God?
2. What have you found to be effective ways of coping with evil? Temptation?
3. How do you view death? Burial procedures?
4. What are your thoughts on the sources of real, deep inner peace of mind?
5. If I were enticed into sin, told you the truth about it and asked your forgiveness, what would be your response?
6. Where do you find your greatest security?
7. What to you are the ingredients of a truly wonderful way of living?

Sex
Questions to Discuss Before or After Marriage
1. Do you feel we are honest and open with each other in talking about sex?
2. Do you feel we have the same standards?
3. What do you feel is the purpose of sex?

Questions to Discuss After Marriage
1. What causes you special pleasure?
2. Do you wish I would initiate sex more often? Less often?
3. How do you feel a woman's moods relate to her menstrual cycle?

Understanding
1. What do you think are my strengths? My weaknesses?
2. How can I best help you when you are depressed?
3. How can I best encourage you? What are ways I am an encouragement to you now? What are ways that I might be?

4. In what areas do you feel I don't understand you?
5. Do you feel you have a true understanding of men? Of women? Do I?
6. How do you see yourself as far as temperament type is concerned? How do you see me?
7. Do you think personalities can be changed? Should be changed?
8. What is your response to a woman crying? To a man crying? To an outburst of temper? What would you like my response to be to these?
9. Who is the most understanding person you have ever known? What about that person makes you say that?
10. Do you feel that I am quick to mention a fault or flaw in you? When I do, do you feel I mean to help? What is your reaction to my suggestions? How could I suggest better?
11. Do you think I sympathize with you at a deep level? With others?
12. What are some ways I can demonstrate that I love you that I am not now doing?
13. What are two of the happiest things that ever happened to you? What brings you the most happiness today?
14. What has been the hardest experience of your life? The saddest? What are the things that cause you the most anxiety today?

Family Backgrounds

1. What were the responsibilities and chores of each family member as you were growing up? How were these accepted by each person? (For example, did they accept them as routine, resent them, gripe about them, try to get out of them?)
2. In your opinion, how should chores for the home, car, lawn, garden, etc., be handled? How should it be decided who does what?
3. What holidays did your family celebrate and how? Which of their traditions do you want to continue in our family? Do you want to add any? How important is this to you? Was Christmas of special importance in your home? How much was spent on gifts?
4. Were table manners and manners in general taught in your home? How diligently? What manners are important to you? (For example, is chewing with one's mouth closed important? Using a knife and fork properly? Opening doors for women? Not interrupting someone who's speaking?)
5. What was your parents' educational background? Was proper English used in your home? How important is the correct use of grammar to you? Is this something you want our family to work on?

6. What events did your family participate in together? Which meals did you eat together as a family? What recreation did you all participate in? Work projects? What did you like about this? Dislike? What would you like our family to do together regularly?

7. What was the general atmosphere around your home? Was there much quarreling, or was it mostly pleasant? Which member of your family did you enjoy being with the most? The least?

8. How important in your home were reunions and getting together with relatives? How important is your extended family to you? How often would you like to see them?

9. How did your family spend vacations? If your family had $300 to spend on a vacation but the house needed painting, would your father have wanted to use that money to paint the house during vacation or go somewhere inexpensive? What about your mother? What would you want to do? What is your ideal vacation on limited funds?

10. What was each member of your family's attitude about God? Church? Spiritual things in general? Which ones were Christians? Who was hostile about spiritual matters? Did you attend church regularly as a family? How committed was your family to that? Did you worship together? Have family devotions? What is your own feeling concerning God, Christ, the Christian life? How do you feel about regular church attendance, and what does "regular" mean to you? What were your families' views concerning Sunday as the Lord's day?

11. What value was held in highest esteem by your father (for example, honesty, integrity, faithfulness, love, kindness)? Your mother? What other values were important, and how was that demonstrated? What values are most important to you, and how would you like to see them worked out in our home?

12. What was the pattern of your family's social life (country club, sports events, big parties, small dinners, games, etc.)? What did you enjoy that you would like to continue? What kinds of things do you dislike?

13. To what extent did your father and mother show an interest in what you were doing? Did they get involved in school activities? Come to events in which you were participating? See that you had your homework done? Of what importance do you think this kind of participation is, and how much should we be involved with our children's activities?

14. What were the rules of conduct in your home? Did you have strict deadlines when you had to be home in the evenings? Rules about

dating? Did your parents insist on knowing where you were most of the time? Did each member of the family keep the others informed of their whereabouts?

15. What was the attitude of your family concerning privacy? Did you walk in and out of bedrooms and/or bathrooms without knocking? What would you like to do in our home concerning this?

16. Was your family conservative or liberal in their thinking? About politics? Religion? What were your families' views on: Abortion? Alcohol? Cigarettes? Drugs? Racial issues?

17. Did your parents teach you about sex? At what age? Was their view of sex healthy? Would you want your children to be raised as you were in this regard? If you didn't learn about sex from your parents, where and what did you learn about it?

18. What kinds of attitudes did your father and mother have concerning money? Were they liberal spenders? Givers? Savers? Did your family operate on a budget? Were they in debt much of the time? If so, from whom did they borrow? Would they be more likely to spend money on new cars, clothes, entertainment, insurance, or other? What were their priorities related to money? Which of their values would you want to emulate? What would you want to avoid?

19. How well do you feel your parents related to one another? To each member of the family? What would you like to carry over from them or avoid?

20. What did your family read? What programs did they watch on television? What kind of movies did they enjoy?

21. What kinds of humor did your family enjoy? (Practical jokes? Puns? Slapstick?)

22. What kinds of pets did your family own? Were they treated as members of the family or kept outside?

23. Did an older relative ever live with your family? What was your parents' attitude toward the widowed or sick and their responsibility toward them?

24. How did your family respond to regular illness (with sympathy, extra caregiving, over concern, ignored it and went on working, etc.)? When you were ill, how did your family treat you? How would you like to be treated?

AUTHORS

JACK AND CAROLE MAYHALL work with the Marriage and Family Ministries of The Navigators.

Jack was raised in Peoria, Illinois, and graduated from Wheaton College (Illinois) and Dallas Theological Seminary. He was ordained in 1954 and served as assistant pastor and youth director at the First Presbyterian Church in Aurora, Illinois, and at Central Bible Church in Portland, Oregon.

Carole graduated from Wheaton College with a degree in Christian education and was the education director at a Columbus, Ohio, church for a year before she married Jack. Carole has written several books including *Words that Hurt, Words that Heal* (NavPress, 1986) and *When God Whispers* (NavPress, 1994).

The Mayhalls joined the Navigator staff in 1956 and Jack has served in various capacities with them, including seven years as the U.S. Director. They have one daughter, Lynn, who is married to Tim Westberg. Tim and Lynn, along with their two children Eric and Sunny (Sonya Marie) serve with the Navigator Missions Department.

This book is based on a seminar on marriage that Jack and Carole have presented throughout the United States and overseas. It has been given to a wide spectrum of groups, including communities, churches, and various conferences.

The Mayhalls can be reached for seminars by writing to 5720 Velvet Court, Colorado Springs, CO 80918.